How to Peel a Sour Grape

How to Peel a Sour Grape

An Impractical Guide to Successful Failure

by RICHARD P. FRISBIE

 Sheed and Ward : New York

Chapters 2, 5, 6, 7, and 10, in somewhat different form, have appeared in *U. S. Catholic*. Acknowledgment is made to Robert E. Burns, the discerning executive editor of *U. S. Catholic*, whose tangible encouragement had much to do with the completion of this book.

Library of Congress Catalog Card Number 65-12197

Manufactured in the United States of America

TO MY WIFE, MARGERY
who has never failed me

Contents

1   Failure Knocks, and Knocks, and Knocks   3

2   In This Asylum, All the Rooms Are Corner Offices   15

3   They're Sawing the Rungs Off the Ladder   33

4   Your Aching Back   49

5   What Kind of Job Is There in This Future?   63

6   Failure by Moonlight   79

7   Termites in the Mahogany   91

8   A Woman's Work Is Never Fun   107

9   Handbook for Husbands   127

10   The Knot in the Filial Tie   139

11   If Your Heart's in the Right Place, Your Foot's in Your Mouth   155

12   How to Fail as a Failure   169

*It is, in fact, not success but failure
that marks man off from the insects.*

M. V. C. JEFFREYS*

* Quoted by permission from *Personal
Values in the Modern World*. Baltimore:
Penguin Books, 1962.

How to Peel a Sour Grape

1

Failure Knocks,
and Knocks, and Knocks

Every man past a certain age, perhaps thirty-five, knows in
his heart that he is a failure. He doesn't realize that almost
everyone else is a failure, too. Romantically, he supposes
success is possible and others have merely succeeded where
he has failed. This delusion is sustained by whole industries
devoted to the production of success symbols and by out-
pourings of books and articles telling how to succeed at
everything from abalone fishing to zoo management. I
think it's time someone snitched. That's why this whole
book is about failure.

There are only three kinds of people: Epic Failures, Dra-
matic Failures, and Romantic Failures. Among the Epic
Failures are men like General George Armstrong Custer,
whose failures have a spectacular quality from which time
and imaginative writers create successful legends. The Dra-
matic Failures are men who deliberately choose the role of
failure so they can get even with their mothers when the

whole sordid story comes out in *True Clinical Psychiatry.*
The rest of us are Romantic Failures.

I don't mind admitting to readers of books that I am, by
and large, a failure. I know you; you're a failure, too, or
you wouldn't have time to read. You'd be too busy being a
success. But before going into that, let me set forth a few of
my innumerable qualifications as an expert on failure.

This is a subject to which I have given considerable
thought. I find that walking from the train to my office in
the morning, a time I could use for thinking of bright,
original ideas to make myself more successful, is instead a
time when my mind tends to dredge up some painful experience from my failure-fraught past. Judging from the
pained expressions on the faces of the other people in the
crowd, brooding over past blunders is a fairly common
morning exercise.

Just the other day, I happened to recall a summer morning when I was five years old. I stole some matches. I put a
few scraps of paper in an empty spaghetti can taken from
the garbage, sat down on the kitchen floor, and set fire to
the paper. I might have succeeded in the experiment without penalty. Or I might have ignited the curtains and created the setting for an Epic Failure. As it happened, after
the paper had flared up and burned away to a crisp ash, I
tried to pick up the can while the metal was still hot. I had
to suffer the pain of a burned hand without even getting to
see the fire engines. Many of my enterprises since have
turned out about the same.

When failures are public, there's usually a better chance
for them to achieve Epic stature. I remember a skit I co-

authored with a friend for our Boy Scout troop parents' night. Each patrol had its own place on the program. The other patrols all took standard skits out of the handbook, rehearsed them, and performed them creditably. My patrol was the only one that insisted on having an original script.

It was so avant garde we didn't understand it ourselves.

With good reason I have forgotten the details. I do remember that it involved a conversation among the Forces of Nature. Since these were invisible, there were no costumes, scenery, or props. In fact, there was no reason to open the school auditorium curtains, so we left them shut while we recited our lines behind them.

Whether the audience would have responded to this drama if our voices had not been muffled by the curtains would be hard to judge after all these years. As it was, they were mystified. My co-author, a Boy Scout named Bernard, peeked through the crack in the curtains during a pause in his portrayal of the Voice of Growing Things. "It's laying an egg," he whispered. "And I've lost the next page. I think you'd better play something quick on your cornet."

Not every playwright keeps a brass band about his person, but I was the troop bugler and had been sitting on my cornet case. I could see Bernard was right about the play. The baffled buzzing of the audience had to be quelled. So I took a breath and played a quavery solo, *My Wild Irish Rose,* with the curtains still drawn. Then the Flaming Arrow Patrol crept into the wings, leaving the audience feeling it had missed something without knowing what, or why. The next act, a silhouette pantomime, was a familiar routine. The audience was relieved to be back on solid ground.

Another fiasco of that period was not only public, it was on network radio. I had been invited to appear on the old Quiz Kids show. In those innocent days, quiz show contestants were not given the answers ahead of time. The only management consisted of selecting questions about subjects in which some of the children were known to be well read. Herpetology was one of my interests at the time. So Joe Kelly, the quizmaster, was quick to call on me when I raised my hand in response to a snake question. The trouble was that I didn't recognize it as having anything to do with snakes.

The question was worded something like this: "Suppose you were walking across a college campus and found a piece of paper on which were written the words 'hoop,' 'carpet,' and 'chain.' In what class might a student have made those notes?"

Kelly expected me to discourse at length on the appearance and habits of carpet and chain snakes, and the nonexistence of the mythical hoop snake. Coast to coast, millions waited for the answer.

I was brilliant. I said, "Embroidery?"

That time there was no cornet to take refuge in.

Some of my best-remembered failures occurred while I was a reporter for the *Chicago Daily News*. (They've been microfilmed for posterity.) I was handicapped by a streak of gullibility. For instance, one night I was assigned to trail a notorious con man who somehow had maneuvered his way out of jail and was appearing on television. With other reporters and photographers, I trudged around to the television studio and various saloons until after midnight. Then the celebrity and his lawyer told us they were going to a certain hotel for the night. I telephoned the city desk, reported the curtain lowered on the spectacle and received permission to return to the office, where I wrote a story for the next day's first edition.

Before going home to bed, I was instructed to leave a note for the day shift, telling them the number of the hotel room where they could pick up the trail in the morning. I phoned the desk clerk at the hotel where the con man was supposed to be staying and asked for the room number. The hotel had never heard of him, which I was obliged to confess to the night city editor.

"But didn't you follow him to the hotel?"

Well, no, I hadn't.

"Then how did you know where he was going?"

"He told me."

"You believed *him?*"

Only then did it occur to me that a confidence artist fresh out of jail was not the most dependable source of information. After his many years of dedication to his profession, he probably couldn't give a straight answer to a question as innocent as "What'll you have?"

I could go on, and I shall. Once, a reader wrote in to tip off the *Daily News* that a certain hamburger palace near a North Side high school was a center for teen-age debauchery. Murder, rape and who knows what other crimes might disturb the tranquillity of the middle-class neighborhood unless someone did something. As the only reporter young enough to pass for a teen-ager, I was ordered to disguise myself with a pullover sweater and a girl friend and investigate.

First, we cruised the neighborhood in my car. (Why not? The paper was paying me 8¢ a mile.) I saw nothing suspicious. No mean-looking kids on the street corners or in the school playgrounds. Then I ventured into the hangout itself and ordered hamburgers. I couldn't help being reminded of all those movies in the thirties with a newspaper reporter hero who befriended a pretty night club singer. She always worked in a night club owned by the gangster who bossed the mob.

But there was no pretty singer in this place. Instead, there was a surly counterman with hairy arms who looked quite capable of dealing with any misbehaving customers. The hamburger had about as much flavor as a policeman's shoe. Not only was it hard to believe that this was a hangout for teen-age hoodlums, it seemed unlikely that anyone would ever return for a bite of the other shoe.

I sought out our faithful reader. He was a young man about my own age who lived with his parents on the quiet side street around the corner from the hangout. A disreputable element, he told me, sat in cars parked in front of his house, drank beer, used naughty language and otherwise indicated a capacity for anti-social activities. Their noise sometimes kept him awake at night, which annoyed him because he rose early to go to work.

When I checked the street, I found three or four cars containing young people as he said. Spying from behind a sticky barberry bush, I could see no illicit goings-on. No beer. Not even any necking. The occupants of the cars seemed to be innocently engaged in conversation.

I interviewed the managers of the nearest theater and the nearest bowling alley, who agreed that they had no more than the usual amount of difficulty with teen-agers. Congratulating myself on my thoroughness, I returned to the office and wrote a report to the city desk stating that the youngsters in question appeared to be wholesome, clean-cut American kids. Our tipster, I said, must be just another busybody.

Within the week, a teen-age brawl in that very hamburger joint had to be put down by four squads of police. It happened on my day off, so it was on the front page of the *Daily News* that I read I had failed again. I was as discouraged as the time I went around to the far side of a warehouse fire just as the firemen began to water down the roof, and got so wet my shoes squished.

I wouldn't want to give the impression that I have specialized as a newspaper failure. Actually, I have been something of a jackass of all trades. When the day came that I was unable to keep our obstetrician in his accustomed style on a newspaper salary, I went to work for an advertising agency. I learned to think in terms of national magazine campaigns and filmed television commercials costing thousands of dollars.

One day, the boss introduced me to a friend from his club who was a contractor specializing in decorating and remodeling commercial buildings. The contractor had an advertising problem, miniscule by ordinary agency standards, but important to us because any problem of a friend of the boss's was a problem of ours. The contractor had been getting leads on jobs to keep his crews busy by mailing mimeographed letters to lists of building and plant managers. A housewife, whose spelling was weak, wrote the letters for him at home in her spare time.

Her letters had been producing five or six inquiries per mailing, but he thought he could do better than that with truly professional help. We agreed. We said we'd give his mailings the Michigan Avenue touch.

After considerable work, an agency art director and I produced a folder for him, with crisp selling copy and a striking two-color design. Something the agency could be proud of.

It failed.

Utterly.

When mailed to a long list of managers, it produced not a single inquiry.

The contractor went back to the semi-literate housewife and his battered mimeograph, which ran smudgy. And the inquiries began trickling in again. The building managers apparently thought they could extort lower bids from a contractor who couldn't get his mimeograph fixed than from one who could afford two-color printing.

Then there was the fund-raising event I directed for a community organization, which fortunately lost only $7. And the floor tile I laid, which still oozes the excess adhesive up through the cracks on hot days. And the walkie-talkie radio kit I am assembling with my eldest son. Only this afternoon, one of his ten-year-old friends sneered at my soldering.

I must admit that to some connoisseurs, like Richard M.

Nixon in 1960, Floyd Patterson, or any player on the New York Yankees of 1963, these failures would seem scarcely more than minor embarrassments, completely lacking the Epic quality. I can only say they looked big enough from close up.

Americans are not conditioned to live gracefully with failure. Dr. Joseph G. Colmen, research director of the Peace Corps, said Peace Corps volunteers generally take about six months to get over the frustration of not being able to achieve immediate success in their work overseas.

> Their achievements, more often than not, have to be measured in psychological terms rather than in the tangible currency of miles of roads built or thousands of bricks laid or hundreds of students taught. For youngsters who have grown up under the American ethic that it's results that count, many of them experience, temporarily at least, a discouraging sense of failure.[1]

Scarcely any of the volunteers, Dr. Colmen added, complain about the difficult living conditions.

It's strange that Americans are so optimistic about success when so few of us ever have much first-hand experience with it. Like the discount store that sells good Scotch for four dollars a fifth, it's always coming up in conversation, but you can never find anyone who has actually been there and can tell you how to find it.

Even those men who seem to have already arrived at a high degree of success could not claim much familiarity with it. So a man is chairman of the board. Secretly, he wishes he were chairman of a bigger company. And he would have been, drat it, but he made a wrong move right after the war. Should have diversified sooner. Or he is a salesman whose sales last year were so high, despite a certain fiasco in Philadelphia, that his boss paid the commissions almost cheerfully. But there are moments of lonely introspection at airport cocktail lounges when the salesman wonders whether he shouldn't have taken the job playing trombone in a jazz band he was offered when he left school.

The world's richest man, J. Paul Getty, has admitted to reporters that life hasn't granted him everything he wished. He mentioned that he would have liked to have been a better conversationalist.[2]

The artist who disdains material goals is no better off in this respect than the most insensitive racketeer. When the artist sits down to work, he believes that this time he'll succeed in creating something worthy of his aspirations. By the time the work is finished, he knows better. And if he's unlucky enough for the work to become popular, he's still worse off. He's not allowed to forget it. Rachmaninoff became so weary of his own most popular music that he couldn't bear to play or hear it. Marlon Brando, a thoughtful actor who won the Academy Award as best actor in 1954, told an interviewer, "Personally, I don't think I am a raging success in my life, nor have I achieved certain things I wanted in the realm of my own soul."[3]

Failure is scarcely a twentieth-century discovery. The first cuss word no doubt was invented by a Stone Age man when he smashed his thumb failing to hammer open a mussel shell. What may be different now is that we feel compelled to conceal our failures from ourselves. A man who fails is perceived not as a brother experiencing the usual lot of mankind but as a pariah, whose ill fortune may be catching. So we surround ourselves with symbols of success and pretend they are the real thing. If someone could invent an after-shave lotion or hair tonic that smelled "successful" instead of like furniture polish, nine out of ten men would be marinated in it.

Small wonder that men grow so weary inside. And their wives, too. The effort to walk around with feet off the ground for a lifetime is grinding. We would be better off if we could cheerfully admit the facts about our failures and go on from there. F. Scott Fitzgerald wrote: "One should . . . be able to see that things are hopeless and yet be determined to make them otherwise."[4]

We don't have to give up trying to achieve the goals we have set for ourselves in this world; we merely should force ourselves to be realistic about the possibilities. Then, when some small success happens along from time to time, we can enjoy it as a refreshing change from the usual state of affairs.

NOTES

1. *New York Times*, June 9, 1963.
2. *Chicago Daily News*, February 25, 1963.
3. "Marlon Brando with Studs Terkel," *Chicago Perspective*, July, 1963.
4. *The Crack-Up*, edited by Edmund Wilson. New York: J. Laughlin, 1945.

2

In This Asylum,
All the Rooms Are Corner Offices

One reason you're a failure is that while you were engaged in the pursuits of normal men—sleeping, taking the kids to the zoo, making love, fishing—someone was gaining on you.

He wasn't sleeping because he has insomnia. He wasn't wasting his time at the zoo because he gets headaches if he doesn't spend most of Saturday at the office. He's neurotic, but now he's your boss.

Being neurotic doesn't make him unusual. An intensive study of mental health in Manhattan revealed that only 18.5 per cent of the population were free enough of emotional symptoms to be considered well. Mild-to-moderate disturbances, such as tensions and nervousness, were reported by 58.1 per cent of the 1,660 persons interviewed over a period of eight years by a team of researchers from Cornell University Medical College. Another 23.4 per cent appeared to be candidates for psychiatric treatment. Pub-

lished under the title, *Mental Health in the Metropolis*,[1]
the Cornell report said these findings were not limited to
Manhattan; they describe much of the urban population of
the country.

The neurotic is popularly thought of as someone who
can't bear to step on the cracks in the sidewalk. (Or, if he's
that kind, can't bear *not* to.) Whatever bothers him, some
built-in emotional maladjustment prevents him from react-
ing to various situations within what is generally considered a "normal" range of behavior. Evidence is accumu-
lating that certain types of neurosis are an asset to the man
who wants to rise to a position of power in one of today's
big organizations.

Many students of organizations and their ways have observed that the men who cluster along the chain of command strongly resemble each other in personality. William
H. Whyte, Jr., added a phrase to the language when he
described this type as "the organization man."[2] In *The
Lonely Crowd*,[3] David Riesman showed that the organization man is "other-directed." A more recent observer of
organizations, Robert Presthus, now divides organization
people into "upward-mobiles," the pure strain which is
admirably bred for bureaucratic in-fighting; "ambivalents,"
who want to get ahead but can't put their hearts in it, and
"indifferents," who buy outboard motor boats to enjoy in
their free time and put the office power struggle out of
their minds.

Presthus, who is professor of public administration at the
Cornell University business school and editor of *Adminis-
trative Science Quarterly*, warns in his book about "the

organizational society"⁴ that the "upward-mobiles" increasingly are gaining control of all kinds of organizations. They are edging out the artists, scientists, engineers, and other highly trained and creative professionals who may be better qualified to make decisions in their own fields but are less adept at organizational maneuvering.

It would be going too far to accuse all successful executives of being—to shorten Professor Presthus' term—pushmobiles. Some are just lucky. Some even rise on irrepressible ability, especially the men at the very top who, in contrast to the bureaucracy around them, can't pass the buck any higher. Nor can all be considered neurotic, which is a range of behavior rather than a clearly defined condition. Nevertheless, the organizational environment requires the surrender of some degree of inner peace from all who come to terms with it.

"Indeed," says Presthus, "an upward-mobile may be roughly defined as one who can take seriously the status systems of big organizations . . . he tends to adore power and is somewhat humorless in his dedication to majority values."⁵

A pushmobile congratulates himself upon moving from an office with a single window to one with two. A three-window office, the next step up, is so much more desirable than a two-window office that the difference is worth $1,000 a year or more in salary. To inhabit a corner office, with four or more windows, is like being knighted and given a castle. (I had a four-window corner office once, but there were no drawers in the desk.) Standard Oil of California classifies executives from type 1, who get private offices with walnut desks, draperies, wall-to-wall carpeting, and suitable accouterments, to type 4, who have to sit at oak desks in shared quarters. A large Chicago advertising agency tried to overcome odious comparisons like this when moving to new quarters by making all the executive offices identical in size and equipment. Very quickly, a new status system sprang up based on such careful calculations as the distance to the elevator.

A stranger unfamiliar with the local executive pecking order can easily tell who's on top by watching to see which executive calls on which during the conduct of the day's business. The subordinate usually goes to his superior's office, where he can be kept waiting for a moment at a psychological disadvantage as a reminder to keep his place.

Let us meet a fictional prototype of the pushmobile. Hector Gladly is working at his desk (mahogany) when an assistant, Henry Strively, enters. Strively has made several intelligent suggestions lately. Fine. But he mustn't be allowed to push ahead too fast. Gripped in the fresh enthusiasm of his latest idea, Strively says, "I think I have the answer to the problem we discussed yesterday. We can—"

Gladly cuts him off. "I'm delighted. But forgive me just a moment. I have to check something with John Beaver." While Strively stands there with his mouth still open, Gladly picks up his phone and dials Beaver, another executive.

"John? This is Heck. Did you get this morning's paper? I see that stock you tried to tout me on is off a couple of points. I just wanted to know whether you have any more good advice for me. Ha. Ha."

Gladly winks broadly at Strively, who is supposed to show his enjoyment of executive humor.

"You're good to offer, John, but I wouldn't think of taking it off your hands. No, I'll let *you* get rich. Well, see you at lunch."

Having been properly cooled off, Strively is then allowed to continue explaining his proposal—if he can remember it.

But suppose it is John Beaver who drops in. Beaver's rank in another department is equal to Gladly's. Gladly follows a different ritual, exhibiting deference toward a fellow mandarin, once pleasantries have been exchanged. Asked the slightest question, Gladly gravely considers it, rises from his desk, paces to the window and looks down briefly from his fortieth-floor window before answering. Pushmobiles are highly sensitive to distinctions of rank, a sensitivity that rubs off on their secretaries. If a girl types the letters of an executive vice president, she is entitled to maintain an imperious tone towards everyone below the rank of department head. Although bad temper nowadays has little career survival value, cold impersonality is allowed to verge on rudeness.

There is an ancient proverb in business: "A good executive wears a worried frown—on the face of his assistant." Something of an overstatement, this saying is nevertheless revealing. At the moment, it is the rationale for a trend in advertising photography intended to sell expensive suits and other products for successful men.

Stephen Baker, *Advertising Age* columnist, reported:

In the past the male model with the toothiest grin got in the picture. . . . Now an applicant is screened on the basis of his facility to scold, squint, wrinkle his nose, turn his mouth down, and appear worried. The more indignant the look, the better.[6]

In the Cornell mental health study mentioned earlier, the researchers found neurotic symptoms associated with rising status. They weren't sure whether men become successful because they are neurotic or become neurotic because they are successful. Either conclusion reveals much about "success" and at least some of the people who enjoy it.

Dr. C. Knight Aldrich, chairman of the University of Chicago psychiatry department, explains why some types of neurotic are better equipped than normal men for business competition.

The man whose past unsolved conflicts add a 'neurotic' component to his basic 'normal' competitive drive has an advantage over his associate. . . . He will work. . . . night and day and over weekends while his better adjusted competitor relaxes with his family. . . . If all other considerations of integrity, tact, intelligence, influence and so on balance out, the man with single-minded devotion to competition wins. His neurotic traits, therefore, pay off in the currency of the American ideal.[7]

Consider the case of John Beaver, a composite push-mobile with extra push. Beaver, despite a fair amount of ability, is inwardly insecure. He doubts his own judgment. He compensates for this by affecting an arrogant and omniscient air, which overawes his subordinates and other business contacts who don't know him well. A perfectionist, he can't work at his desk unless his secretary has laid out his pencils parallel to the edge of the blotter. That's one reason he is always breaking in a new secretary. His perfectionism gives him an excuse to make his subordinates revise their work over and over. Not feeling certain in his assessment of the results, he tells himself that if they do it over enough times they can't help getting it right in the end.

His perfectionism might be a handicap, but he more than makes up for any excess fussing by working long hours. Even when he goes away for a vacation trip, he takes work with him. He packs a whole suitcase with memos, reports, and business correspondence to read.

He likes to give parties he can dominate, but he's ill at ease as a guest at someone else's party. He is not popular. This is tragic because he secretly craves the very affection and admiration from which his overbearing approach to others cuts him off.

However, when he gains the advantage on someone in the competitive organizational world, he forgets the psychic bruises acquired in other areas of life. His response to an assortment of disappointments is to devote even more time to his job, the source of his chief pleasure.

"Home for the neurotic competitor," says Dr. Aldrich, "represents either no competition, which bores him; a handicap to his competitive efforts, which makes him nervous; or an alternative competitive field."[8]

Beaver has an ulcer. This is less a badge of success than generally supposed, since relaxed people also get ulcers. But when a competitive neurotic gets one he's especially difficult to treat. He won't slow down. He didn't get ahead of the pack by taking it easy, did he? Besides, the other wolves are just waiting for a chance to close in on him. It's against his nature to accept advice from anyone, even his doctor.

A Kaiser Foundation research project uncovered hundreds who were problem patients like Beaver. Instead of admitting they needed help, they felt impelled to deny their symptoms. They tried to persuade their doctors that they actually felt fine.[9]

Dr. Aldrich has devised a method that sometimes is successful with a hard case like Beaver. He tries to engage the neurotic in competition against the other ulcer patients. Beaver's doctor tried this reverse psychology on him, and it worked. Now Beaver follows directions faithfully, aided by his new secretary (she's ideal for him—another neurotic perfectionist). He's determined to show up the other ulcer patients. He secretly reads several medical journals, picking up bits of information with which he hopes to show up his doctor, too, when the opportunity occurs.

Beaver hates to lose at anything: tennis, golf, speeding away from stoplights. Many of his colleagues are able to accept defeat gracefully in marginal matters. They reserve all their competitive drive for the office, and would have to be described as "overmotivated" rather than "compulsive."

These are generalizations, of course, which can never completely describe the complex personality of an individual. Generalizations can't account for the compulsive who is relaxed on Mondays—at least till noon—because his wife makes his weekends at home so pleasant. Or for the successful pushmobile whose basic decency comes to the fore at critical moments. The usefulness of generalizations is in describing trends and making them concrete enough to discuss. The generalizations in this essay are based on recent findings of sociological and psychological research, only slightly perverted by my own observations of the organizational scene. They apply especially, in Presthus's phrase, to "authoritarian occupations such as business, medicine, the military, police work, and religion."[10]

With this in mind, let us turn to the family album of Hector Gladly, typical pushmobile. As a child, Hector discovered that persuading others to do things came easily to him. Not only did he have a knack for it, but it also gave him a sense of well-being. There on the third page is a snapshot of Hector in high school. He must have been talking when the shot was made because his mouth is open and the lower jaw is blurred.

Hector worked up to his present position with the Interplanetary Corporation without having worked anywhere else. (In 1900, two-thirds of major business executives had had independent experience. In 1950, only 11 per cent could make this claim, and 22 per cent had never had a job with any other company.)[11] Possibly, this is why Hector acts as if he were overcompensating for secret moments of self-doubt and insecurity. He makes a point of letting it be known that he is a rock of strength rising from the sea of weaklings that surrounds him. Young people would be tougher, he says, if they had more experience with strict discipline. In the family photo album is a recent picture of Hector at the rostrum, addressing an executives' meeting. Among other remarks typical of such occasions, he said:

"What this country needs most, more than laws or political programs, is a few courageous, tireless, devoted leaders in whom the people can put their faith."

Hector enjoys using words like "strength" and "discipline." The ring of them makes him feel like a "tireless leader" himself. Self-deception is another common trait of the pushmobile.

In the Kaiser Foundation project, each of a group of executives was asked to rate himself on a personality scale. Then each executive rated his colleagues. The two sets of personality profiles did not match. One production manager, for example, said he was "strong" and "somewhat friendly," while his associates described him as "extremely cold, hard, unfriendly, selfish."[12]

Successful executives tend to feel an intense personal attachment to their superiors while looking down on their assistants impersonally as mere doers of work. This makes it hard to tell what a man is really like. There are always three competing versions: his own, that of his boss, and that of the boys in the back of the department, which is likely to prove the most accurate.

Although pushmobiles vie with each other for power, they band together against outsiders. In every organization, there are some men who want to climb without paying the price. They balk at corporate discipline and demands for conformity. They are unwilling to sit patiently through endless meetings, endure committee work with incompetents, and make the many other sacrifices that are part of the folkways of bureaucracy. True pushmobiles don't understand these nonconformists, resent their attempts to enjoy the best of two worlds, and automatically work with each other to keep the nonconformists where they can't cause trouble.

Despite his problems, the pushmobile rather enjoys his work. He should. His reward for playing the organization's game is a generous share of the power, income, and ego-reinforcement the organization has to dispense. In fact, even those men who are capable of creative work are encouraged by the incentive system to become pushmobiles instead; it pays better.

Once, prestige was acquired through accomplishment. Now it exists independently. As long as Beaver and Gladly occupy their offices and collect their salaries, they enjoy high prestige whether they do anything or not. Of course, prestige that depends solely on victories in the intramural pushmobile race can vanish with the first defeat. That's why pushmobiles don't like to take risks.

Here is another photo in Gladly's album, showing him waving from the door of the company plane. He is returning from an important policy meeting with several division managers and the research director. A turbulent meeting. Interplanetary Corporation is burdened with a research director who is more of a scientist than a pushmobile. He fights for a course of action because he believes in it for its own sake. Gladly, who didn't get where he is today by backing lost causes, considers him incredibly unsophisticated. Gladly and several other executives would like to force the research director out of the company, but his work has been so spectacularly successful that at the moment they don't dare.

Outstanding talent will always find its place. That's part of the definition of genius. But many persons with considerable ability, who deserve better, are being held down. In many fields, where skill used to be enough, conformity is now considered more important. The men at the top who decide such matters as promotions often know little about the skills required for the myriad complex operations under their control. They do easily recognize the kind of man in whose hands they can place a fraction of their own power without fearing that he'll use it against them.

A remark by a government security officer has become famous as a summary of this point of view: "An ounce of loyalty is worth a pound of brains."[13]

The chairman of Interplanetary Corporation recently delivered the commencement address at a university which simultaneously conferred on him an honorary degree. His text was the increasing need for "creativity" in business. Meanwhile, back at the office, the few surviving idealists, nonconformists, and creative mavericks were being massacred. The chairman should have told the graduates that even the kind of young man who once would have been advised to woo the boss's ugly daughter now would be better off to cultivate a compulsive-competitive neurosis.

Because researchers have found neurotics so much more interesting, not much is known about "normal" men. One study of mentally healthy college students revealed their chief common trait to be the absence of a burning desire to gain riches, social prestige, or fame. Many of them were preparing for careers that would be socially useful—and low-paid.[14] Another study indicated that emotional stability comes more easily to the sons of successful men. They apparently don't lie awake nights worrying about how to get ahead; they take it for granted that they'll automatically take over Father's locker at the country club.[15]

Does this mean mental health can be achieved only at the cost of ambition and creativity? The researchers were not prepared to state such a broad conclusion—wisely, since terms like "normal" and "success" are so difficult to define.

Significantly, countless workers, both white-collar and blue-collar, have consciously chosen not to compete against the pushmobiles at their own game. They suspect that decisions affecting their progress are made by personages so remote in the organization hierarchy that there's no hope any longer of catching the boss's eye with nothing more than a well-done job. And they are right. The trend now is for the workers to remain forever the workers and management to fall when ripe from the branches of the Harvard Business School.

Is it more "normal" to accept the reality of such a situation or to delude yourself with largely fictional expectations? Men who remain indifferent to organizations and their myths at least escape mistaking organization life for a sort of religion. Successful pushmobiles, having dedicated so much of themselves to the organization in return for its rewards, must rationalize their actions. This takes the form of turning the organization into a Larger Cause worthy of sacrifice. Individuals may make mistakes, but the organization is assumed to be always right and always just.

"The organization tends to resemble a church," says Robert Presthus, "which needs champions to endorse its values and increase its survival power. No dissenters need apply."[16] The pushmobile is no dissenter. In serving the good of the organization, he is able to rise above considerations like loyalty to friends or personal ideals.

Anyone in business can cite numerous examples. The pushmobiles at a Chicago company fired two executives while they were in the hospital. (One wonders what bedside manner the bearer of the tidings assumed.) In another company, a veteran employee was fired, not because of any deficiency in his work, which continued good, but because the management found a younger man whose ability seemed comparable. The younger man, being less experienced, would work for a lower salary.

Any pushmobile would say: "Of course, they canned the old guy. He was obviously overpaid. You have to run a tight ship to stay in business these days." Idealists, of whom some fortunately survive in positions of influence, would say: "Rather than do things like that to stay in business, I'll nail my colors to the mast and go down with glory."

Ten-second questionnaire:

1. Which kind of person is more likely to be held up as a splendid example for emulation by the young?

2. Which kind of person is more likely to continue rising in an organization?

Hector Gladly would tell you that the peculiarities of big organizations are justified by their efficient production of goods and services for society. But this common assumption can't be proved, and anyone who has dealt with organizations has his doubts. Although it's true that automobiles or steel could scarcely be manufactured in a garage workshop, the biggest plant isn't necessarily the most efficient. "Belief in the 'efficiency' of bureaucratic organization is almost impossible to sustain," says Presthus.[17] In one well-known steel company, to obtain authorization for special marketing projects down the chain of command used to require more than a year by the time the various points of view were resolved. Cameron Hawley, another well-known observer of organizations, declares: "Our inability to compete in world markets today is much less a matter of higher labor costs than it is of the excessive load of overhead with which so many American corporations have burdened themselves."[18]

Many social critics see the highest cost of this state of affairs in the subtle corrosion of the individual's integrity. So many of us are constantly engaged in professional manipulation of others that we trust no one. Almost every human contact begins with the assumption on both sides that the other guy is being nice only because he wants to use you in some way. There's not much chance for developing warm "I-Thou" relationships when you can't tell whether your working companions are patting you on the back or feeling for your wallet.

Personal integrity suffers also through the organization's diffusion of responsibility. It would be unfair to make too much of the similarity between Nazi Germany and existing large organizations; the latter, after all, are engaged in the relatively innocent pursuit of making money while providing corner offices for executives. But the justification for the Nuremberg Trials was that every person is morally responsible for his acts. If this principle is slipping away from us in business and other organizations, who can guess what horrors might result?

Pushmobiles instinctively protect themselves by avoiding independent decisions. When something goes wrong, it is often impossible to find anyone to blame because the decision was spread around among so many individuals. Which is just the way they like to operate.

When Clarence B. Randall returned to his office at Inland Steel after a tour of duty in government service a few years ago, he saw the business world with fresh eyes. He recorded his surprise at the prevalence of "intense preoccupation with problems of self."[19] This is an authentic statement of the basic problem of the pushmobile, who may be paying a psychic rent for his corner office that's higher than you could afford.

NOTES

1. L. Srole and others, *Mental Health in the Metropolis, Vol. I.* New York: McGraw-Hill, 1962.

2. William Hollingsworth Whyte, *The Organization Man.* New York: Simon & Schuster, 1956.

3. David Riesman with Nathan Glazer and Reuel Denney, *The Lonely Crowd.* New Haven: Yale University Press, 1950.

4. Robert Presthus, *The Organizational Society: An Analysis and a Theory.* New York: Knopf, 1962.

5. *Ibid.*

6. *Advertising Age,* June 10, 1963.

7. Address to Executive Program Club, Sherman House, Chicago, February 21, 1963.

8. *Ibid.*

9. Timothy Leary, *Interpersonal Diagnosis of Personality.* New York: Ronald Press, 1956.

10. Presthus, *op. cit.*

11. *Ibid.*

12. Leary, *op. cit.*

13. Presthus, *op. cit.*

14. Roy Grinker, Sr., Roy Grinker, Jr., John Timberlake, *AMA Archives of General Psychiatry,* August, 1962.

15. *New York Times,* April 1, 1963.

16. Presthus, *op. cit.*

17. *Ibid.*

18. *Life,* June 2, 1961.

19. Henry F. Graff, "Decease of the Log Cabin Legend," *New York Times Magazine,* June 30, 1963.

3

They're Sawing
the Rungs Off the Ladder

There are people in the world who would kick a cocker spaniel out of sheer meanness, but I have never heard of anyone depraved enough to give a pessimistic commencement address. Of course, people who kick cocker spaniels seldom are invited to be commencement speakers. If they were, I think the sight of all those bright, eager young faces would appeal to their better natures. As surely as the mail must go through and the show must go on, one must speak to the young of widening horizons and endless opportunities.

Immature and untried, the young are not ready for the truth, which is that most of them are mediocrities now and will be mediocrities all their lives. (Like the rest of us.) Mediocrity has its advantages. You don't have to worry about being jostled on the street by autograph seekers. Burglars aren't much of a threat to your meager possessions. And you can keep your old friends.

Still, speakers and writers are expected to exhort everyone, young and old, to set no limit to aspiration. This official optimism is considered a form of public service that helps preserve the human race from despair. I wonder. An excess of optimism could also be a foolish flight from reality that serves only to make us unnecessarily discontent.

Asked about vocational plans, many young persons immediately mention one of the glamorous occupations. They want to be actors, airline pilots, artists, photographers, reporters, writers, and such, with certainty that fame and wealth will be easily attained. What are their chances? Browsing through available figures on employment indicates that anyone who has made any progress at all in any field is already beating the odds against him.

In the whole country, there are fewer than 20,000 actors and actresses.[1] Most of them are hungry. A few hundred are "stars" with a popular following and large incomes. Others do fairly well with the help of television and radio commercial assignments. Theatrical unions estimate the annual incomes of the majority at less than $2,500.

Airline pilots enjoy good pay, averaging about $17,500 a year, but have to compete for a limited number of jobs. In 1962, the U.S. Bureau of Labor Statistics listed only 13,500. During the next several years, because of the large passenger-capacity of jets, few additional jobs are expected. At this rate, there are enough small boys in my neighborhood who want to fly to supply the nation with pilots for a generation.

It isn't only youth that longs for a glamorous life's work. Many a staid businessman inwardly wishes he'd taken up a different occupation. Art, for instance. Some artists manage to work full-time at it. Illustrators may get as much as $4,000 for a national magazine cover. Art directors in well-established advertising agencies make $15,000 to $20,000 a year. But again, the openings are limited—sustaining only about 50,000 commercial artists of all kinds, including free-lancers. And $100 to $125 a week is their usual pay.

Encouraged by today's automatic cameras that take over the thinking, amateur photographers sometimes wish they could have made a profession of their favorite hobby. If they had started young and worked hard, they could have been one of the 55,000 photographers now snapping pictures, mostly for $165 a week or less. For every photographer who works with beautiful models or public figures, there are scores taking baby photos and wedding snapshots.

Having been a newspaper reporter, I can testify that half the people a reporter interviews in the line of duty wish they had his job. Some envy the influence of the press in public affairs, others are thrill-seekers. They don't know that the average reporter has less influence than a precinct captain. They don't know how tedious are most of the speeches and public hearings that a reporter has to sit through. They forget about the unpleasantness of working close to the fringes of society.

One summer evening I stood in an old dirt-floored tool shed while the police dug up the body of a man killed several days before by a neighbor in a drunken brawl. As they say at Irish wakes, he didn't look like himself. When I went to his home for more information, I found that his relatives didn't yet know he was dead. I had to tell them.

In positions to enjoy "excitement" like this are 25,000 to 30,000 reporters working for daily and weekly newspapers and other newsgathering organizations. Like other occupations, glamorous or not, being a reporter offers a mixed bag of disadvantages and advantages. In general, it doesn't pay especially well. In 1960, the relatively few reporters who managed to land jobs on papers with circulations above 150,000 were averaging $8,705 after six or more years of experience.

No one knows how many free-lance writers there are. Thousands, including well-known and successful authors, hold full-time jobs in other fields. Edward Streeter, whose best-selling humorous books began with *Dere Mabel* in 1919, was a banker for twenty-five years before deciding only recently to write full-time. Looking at a display of newly issued books in a book store, I mentally checked off the occupations of the authors familiar to me. The group included a college professor, a magazine editor, a book-store operator, a newspaper columnist, and two housewives. No full-time free-lancers. Most estimates agree that there are no more than a couple of hundred full-time free-lance writers making a comfortable middle-class living. One authority, W. C. Lord, reports that 71.3 per cent of published American authors earn less than $5,000 a year by writing, 50 per cent less than $1,600.[2]

Traditionally, a bright young man who aspired to a socially useful career that would give him considerable personal freedom and a good income was advised to enter one of the professions. Although this is still good advice, the obstacle course is being lengthened.

The 250,000 lawyers are perhaps too numerous for their

own good. In metropolitan centers, it is difficult for a young lawyer to establish an independent practice without influential connections. Many have to take salaried jobs with government or business, and starting salaries of $6,000 to $6,500 look good to them. Salaries rise with experience, but in a 1954 survey only 5 per cent of the lawyers reported making more than $25,000 a year.[3]

For most of the 250,000 physicians, a good income is assured. A 1955 survey placed the median income of family doctors at $15,000. One-third made $20,000 or more.[4] However, medical schools are notoriously picky in accepting applicants. Considerable financial backing is needed to carry students through school and the lean early years of practice. Once established, doctors tend to take the money for granted and yearn for professional recognition from their colleagues, an aspect of the success struggle I'll deal with later.

In the scholarly occupations, everyone knows that substantial financial returns, rare enough in any field, are nonexistent. Persons with scholarly leanings hope the study of archaeology, astronomy, physics, or whatever branch of knowledge attracts them, will offer a comfortable living to at least a few of the more eminent scholars. What is not generally realized is how few. Physicists, not counting several thousand employed in the special field of atomic energy, number only 35,000, although physics is one of the most rapidly expanding branches of science and the best paid. Median income for physicists with fifteen to nineteen years' experience is about $14,000. That looks like big money indeed to scholars in most other fields.

Astronomy, despite growing interest in space, provides

only about 1,000 jobs with a median annual salary of
$9,000. Archaeology, combined with ethnology and all the
other branches of anthropology, employs only about 1,500.
(A few archaeologists do get to go on expeditions to look
for buried artifacts, but with your luck you wouldn't find
anything when you got there.) Archaeologists survive on
typical museum and university salaries, which range downward from the average of $9,262 paid a full professor in
1960-61 in four-year colleges.

All the occupations mentioned so far are special cases,
accounting for a small percentage of the labor force. The
real business of America is still business. Census reports list
more than seven million managers, proprietors, and executives.[5] (Farm proprietors not included.) Obviously, this
category is loosely defined. Going to work in shirt and tie
makes you a white-collar worker; in some businesses, if the
shirt is clean, you're an executive.

Regardless of definitions, you probably knew all along
that at least seven million competitors were trying constantly to keep you in your place, or take away the place
you already have.

The average compensation for the chief executives of
1,157 companies in a 1961 survey ranged downward from
$91,000 in manufacturing to only $53,000 in life insurance.[6] Hordes of minor business functionaries, considered
members of the executive staff, actually make less than
$8,000.[7] Our 500 largest industrial corporations alone have
nine million employees. For these nine million, as for most
others, the odds against rising to the top are stiff.

Few executives can consider themselves successful without reservation. Oddly, being the head of a large corpora-

tion doesn't make you rich. The editors of the *Wall Street Journal* estimate the total number of millionaires in the country at 17,000 to 30,000.[8] Scarcely any of them grew wealthy on an executive salary. The rare executive making $200,000 a year has to pay $156,820 in federal income taxes, leaving him with take-home pay approximately equal to the interest on a million dollars conservatively invested. Almost the only way to amass a fortune today is through ownership of business property which greatly increases in value.

In such a case, the owner pays only the capital-gains tax if he sells his holdings. If he doesn't sell, taxes are paid only on the current income produced by the property; its vast increase in value remains untaxed. (That, in one paragraph, is the most important fact to remember if you'd just as soon be rich as the way you are.)

Unfortunately, starting in business for yourself has never before been so difficult, except perhaps in the depths of major recessions. The trend to centralization has made enterprise in basic industries far from free for individuals. Estimates of the minimum capital needed to set up an efficient, competitive plant range upwards from half a million dollars in shoe manufacturing to $225 million for an automobile plant and $665 million for a steel mill.[9] In 1910, 23 per cent of the work force was self-employed. By 1959, only 15 per cent enjoyed this freedom.[10] The entrepreneurial spirit survives, but few new businesses do. The 1963 bankruptcy rate was the highest in history.

In service businesses, for which relatively little capital is required, established operators gang up to keep newcomers out. They organize an association which lobbies for a state law requiring licensing. Then the association writes a list of qualifications and an examination each applicant must pass before receiving a license. Ostensibly, this system protects the public from poorly qualified practitioners, as it does in such professions as medicine and dentistry. But in many service occupations it is a transparent device to inhibit competition.

Now there's talk in public relations circles about certifying public relations men who pass an examination in p.r. techniques and knowledge of business generally. Advocates piously point to the desirability of upholding ethical standards. Scoffers say the kind of "unethical" conduct the certifiers most want to prevent is account kidnaping. They're trying to make it harder for an account executive to leave with his account, rent an office across the street, and set up his own shop.

Competitive strains extend even to occupations not ordinarily associated with jostling and back-stabbing. The U.S. Agricultural Extension Service has warned farm boys that most of them won't be able to cut the mustard in the mustard fields. "Nine out of every ten of our present crop of farm-reared boys have no other choice than to find off-farm employment," said an Extension Service report.[11]

The notion that the United States is a rich country is partly a myth. Although we are well-off compared to undeveloped nations, the lavish standard of living depicted in movies, television, and advertising is fictional. In 1961, according to the U.S. Department of Commerce, of 56.6 million families, only 3.7 million attained an income above $15,000 a year. Only 9.9 million made $10,000 or more.

Comment in the press until the recent discovery of poverty tended to crow about the well-fixed 9.9 million and the market they represent for all kinds of goods and services. But what about the other 46.7 million? With a normal number of children to educate, old folks to support, medical bills to pay, roofs to replace, and other financial crises to meet, even the families that appear comfortably middle-class by comparison with the truly poor are never more than a couple of paychecks from disaster.

In upper-income groups, the Joneses are almost never as affluent as you think they are. It's human nature for the living room to be nicely furnished while up in the children's room the dresser has to be propped up with books. You drive by a manorial house and visualize its interior as including a paneled study with a fireplace. You don't know that the owner is at that moment pacing the study trying to figure out how he can pay the taxes on it if he has the exterior painted this year, or vice versa.

Dr. Lloyd Ohlin of the U.S. Department of Health, Education and Welfare blames the myth of affluence for contributing to delinquency among the youth of minority groups. Television, he says, usually portrays the good life in materialistic terms.[12] Young Negroes and other members of underprivileged groups become frustrated and bitter as they realize that the standard of living seen on the screen is beyond their grasp. They have no way of knowing that few Americans live in studio-set splendor, that while life is somewhat better on the right side of the tracks Ma hasn't had a new coat in four years and the car needs tires.

You can accomplish anything if you try hard enough,

says the commencement tradition, reinforced by countless books about inner dynamics and assorted methods for increasing your stature, cubit by cubit, through positive thinking.

This is a harsh judgment on millions who are willing to work but start out with handicaps. Despite recent progress, a dark skin is enough to prevent an employee from rising to the top of American Telephone and Telegraph, for instance, over the heads of 745,000 others. What about all the people, black and white, who aren't especially brilliant?

The well-tempered commencement speaker passes over the subject of individual differences with a quick glissando. He may draw inspiration from Theodore Roosevelt, who became a national symbol of vigor by determinedly building his health after a sickly youth, or from Edwin H. Land, who revolutionized photographic technology through dogged research after leaving Harvard without his bachelor's degree. It would be undemocratic and outrageous to admit that in such cases unusual abilities accompany unusual persistence.

But in every field, certain inborn advantages put a fortunate few out ahead from the beginning. Perfect pitch is a priceless help to a singer or a musician. Speed and natural agility increase your potential for Olympic medals. If you're big, good-looking, and have a personality that projects half a block, no skinny introvert is likely to get your job. Unless, of course, the skinny introvert is the only son of the chief stockholder—an inborn advantage that's hard to beat.

Social classes are becoming more fixed in this country

than they used to be. The day is already past when a man could begin as a worker in the plant and work up to the executive offices. Having the right family connections and attending the right schools mean more now than years ago when the President of the United States himself might have been born in a log cabin. This is evidenced by numerous trends.

Language, to mention one. The "write-like-youse-talk" faction among English specialists enjoys rising influence. Schools have always had trouble bringing pupils to terms with correct language, but at least they used to try. Now educators are told that the concept of "correct" language is old-fashioned, pedantic, and undemocratic.

Lincoln Barnett, a respected magazine writer and author, has charged:

> Again and again in the writings of the linguistic philosophers there appears the leitmotiv that language should not be corrected or refined, that everybody should continue to talk the way his parents did, and that any teacher who tries to improve a student's language is endangering the latter's pysche and morale.[13]

Consequently, children of meagerly educated parents continue to speak and write in language that immediately sets them apart from the children who have always heard English spoken at home more or less correctly. A powerful contribution to class rigidity.

Suppose a company hires two boys to work in the stock room. Although business nowadays prefers its recruits fresh-minted from college, advancement from the stock room via hard work and night school is not yet impossible for high school graduates. On the first day, the boss comes staggering through the stock room with an armload of tax records. The first boy ignores him. The second boy cheerfully springs to his side, saying, "Leave me help you with them things." Instead of being favorably impressed by the boy's alert, positive attitude, the boss notices his manner of speech and writes himself a mental memo that the stock room is where this kid belongs.

There are many reasons why progress in a career may require more of an individual than the optimistic tradition has led him to expect. If he marries early and acquires children, he may not be able to hold out in one of the slow-starting professions. Maybe his health won't stand up to a steady diet of business-luncheon martinis, airline flight dinners, and other vicissitudes of executive life. His personality may include a streak of independence that prevents him from fitting smoothly into the Organization.

A large number of organizations still use personality tests as a basis for hiring. Conformists generelly do well while the most intelligent and creative applicants find it difficult to give by-the-book answers to asinine questions. ("Would you rather attend a baseball game or a symphony concert?" And they don't tell you who's playing.) So you can be too bright for your own good as well as not bright enough.

Perhaps you were not made to devote your time and energy unflaggingly to narrow interests. In studying a group of new millionaires, the editors of the *Wall Street Journal* found that these otherwise individualistic persons tended to have traits in common which most of us lack.[14]

One was a willingness to take risks most men with family responsibilities would consider imprudent. Another was capacity for single-minded attention to business beyond the powers of anyone with broad interests. Usually, they also possessed some particular knack that could be translated readily into cash.

Thomas F. Bolack, oil millionaire, spent three penniless years prospecting for oil in a wilderness area where geologists agreed no oil would ever be found. They were wrong. Bolack, who apparently can smell oil through a couple of thousand feet of solid rock, was right.

Peter Kanavos, who made his millions in real estate, has a flair for visualizing shopping centers and other developments in the midst of a swamp. He has equal flair for persuading zoning authorities, bankers, tenants, and other interested parties to see the same vision. "He could talk a dog down from a meat cart," said an associate.[15]

Winston J. Shuler, millionaire restaurateur, works fifteen hours a day, seven days a week. He remembers thousands of patrons and greets them by name. He says, "I have so much fun out of the job that I've never had to look for a hobby, join a country club or anything like that."[16]

Work yields various kinds of satisfaction. Money heads the list only because it is tangible. It helps define the various degrees of failure with mathematical precision, which is possibly a more important use of money than converting it into comforts and possessions. However, the occupational world offers plenty of opportunity for not getting ahead in non-monetary ways.

Artists, musicians, writers, and teachers are among those who derive keen satisfaction from knowing in their hearts

that they are meeting standards they have set for themselves. But this type of person tends to keep raising the
standards just enough to keep himself dissatisfied and
touchy.

In the arts, critical acceptance can be solacing, especially
when recognition from the unlettered public is not forth-
coming. If the critics like it, public taste may catch up in a
few years. Unfortunately, professional critics are notorious
for not liking much. The artist who depends for satisfaction entirely on the applause of the critics is likely to have a
sour disposition.

In the scholarly occupations, the satisfaction of recognition by peers comes from having articles accepted by
learned journals and winning appointment to the faculties
of leading universities. Both represent victory over persist-
ent and cunning competition. There are about 2,000 colleges and universities, of which only a handful possess
enough prestige to rub off on the faculty. And among the
200,000 full-time college and university teachers, only a
few, after ten or fifteen years of trying, can win appointment as full professors anywhere, prestigeful college or
otherwise.

In general, the pay is low in occupations that rate high in
intrinsic satisfaction, like teaching exceptional children.
This is because of the first principle of economics: the size
of your slice varies in inverse proportion to your distance
from the point at which the melon is sliced up. A paleontologist has to love paleontology for its own sake, but an
advertising man can retire young and go into politics like
Chester Bowles.

Whatever the field, it's hard to face the fact that you haven't progressed as far in twenty or thirty years of trying as you intended when you started. Looking at your chances realistically, which is the point of this chapter, may help you resist the temptation to despair or self-recrimination. Why blame yourself for having failed to attain goals that, in reality, were always impossibly remote anyway?

That's the real message of the commencement speaker who tells us to lift our eyes to the stars.

NOTES

1. Unless otherwise noted, figures on employment and income in this chapter are taken from *Occupational Outlook Handbook*, U. S. Bureau of Labor Statistics, Bulletin No. 1300, 1961, and Bulletin No. 1375, 1963.

2. *Saturday Review*, May 2, 1964.

3. S. Dolores Branche, ed., *Handbook of Job Facts* (2nd ed.), Chicago: Science Research Associates, 1959.

4. *Ibid.*

5. *U. S. Statistical Abstracts*. Washington, D.C.: Government Printing Office, 1960.

6. *Top Executive Compensation*, Studies on Personnel Policy No. 186, New York: National Industrial Conference Board, 1962.

7. Branche, *op. cit.*

8. *The New Millionaires and How They Made Their Fortunes*, New York: Bernard Geis, 1961.

9. Joseph Bain, "Economics of Scale, Concentration and Entry," *American Economic Review*, Vol. 44, p. 37.

10. W. S. Woytinski and associates, *Employment and Wages in the United States*, New York: Twentieth Century, 1953.

11. *New York Times*, August 25, 1963.

12. *Science News Letter*, June 9, 1962.

13. "Who Is Behind the Assault on English?" *Horizon*, July, 1963.

14. *Op. cit.*

15. *Ibid.*

16. *Ibid.*

4

Your Aching Back

I am thinking out this page lying in a chaise longue in my backyard on a sunny afternoon. Being a writer, I am working, although I certainly don't look like it to my neighbors, who no doubt are wondering why I don't do something about the weeds along the back fence. Around the world, others are working under different circumstances. Migrant farm laborers stooping in the fields, backs aching, straining to make a little extra money today against the coming winter. Suburbanites stooping over their lawns in the same posture but sustained in their labors by the thought of the highball being prepared in the kitchen. Navajo artisans setting turquoise in silver. Clerks recording transactions on the New York Stock Exchange. Miners sweating in the diamond mines of South Africa. Professors advising students to try a different major. Naked Indians spearing fish in the tributaries of the Amazon. Public relations men taking editors to lunch. Assemblers soldering connections in a television factory. Priests dictating letters in the Vatican.

On a yacht cruising the Mediterranean, the owner of several companies writes out orders to be shortwaved to his office in London. In a swamp in India, a herpetologist is catching frogs. In a ball park in Tokyo, Japanese baseball players are catching flies.

Amid such variety, it is difficult to focus on the universal concept, Man-at-work. Am I in my chaise longue working in the same sense as an Indian coolie hauling dirt in a basket on his back to build a dam? Both of us are earning our daily bread through "the sweat of our faces," although the coolie sweats so much more for so much less profit that it's embarrassing to think about. There is another difference. Freed from economic necessity, I would continue to write. But I'm quite certain that if the coolie suddenly turned out to be the missing heir of a rich maharajah he would never pick up another basketful of dirt in his life.

Work occupies most of mankind's waking hours during most of life. Why is it a joy for some and a curse for others? We can see the problem more clearly if instead of trying to figure out what kind of work a tycoon is doing when he telephones instructions to his broker we imagine an earlier and simpler stage in the growth of society.

We now encounter Independent Man, a prosperous farmer and craftsman who raises his own food; makes his own clothing, shelter, and tools; and provides his own amusements. Happy and secure, with a full barn, he leads a life containing the elements which, under favorable conditions, put work in equilibrium with the needs of human nature. Since he is a composite figure we can overlook the realities of human history and ignore the poor health, weak character, bad weather, crop failure, invading armies, and other disasters which always have kept most people poor and miserable.

Independent Man exults in facing a variety of challenges to mind and body from day to day. He plans ahead to have his seed and equipment ready at the right planting time. He decides about the disposition of crops when they're harvested. Through observation, he grows increasingly expert in the care of his animals. His body is constantly exercised, lifting, digging, hoeing, rhythmically swinging tools such as the scythe, pulling on ropes attached to recalcitrant calves, sprinting after loose chickens. He invents tools, makes and repairs them, and in an occasional burst of creativity decorates the handles with carved symbols of the beneficent forces of nature.

He is responsible for his own decisions. He and his family may suffer if he is a poor decision-maker, but when he is right he knows a satisfaction reserved in our industrial society for a few top managers. When a decision is moral as well as practical, like whether to eat a neighbor's goose that strayed into his field, the full blame or credit is his, with no directives from superiors to confuse the issue.

Within limits, he chooses his work. He can often arrange to work outdoors when the weather is inviting. A cold, rainy spell finds him overhauling equipment next to a warm fire or whittling wooden animals for the children. If he goes out in a blizzard to rescue livestock, however reluctantly, he goes freely. Men will volunteer to do things for themselves that no one could make them do except at spearpoint.

He controls his work. Contrary to the attitude of some modern managers, a man is not a machine that produces an equal amount of work hour after hour, day in and day out. Each man has an individual pace. One starts vigorously in the morning and gradually slows down. Another fumbles around in the morning, but finishes strong in the afternoon. Organized types like to schedule their days, half the work before lunch, half after. Impulsives prefer to tackle a job in the middle, work furiously in all directions for ten or twelve hours to finish it, then knock off for a day or two and go fishing.

The main reason industry employs industrial relations experts is to mitigate the problems raised when the machine pace of the industrial environment forces men to work with unnatural rhythms. Instead of deploring high absentee rates, industry should be grateful that the rate isn't 100 per cent on soft spring days.

Besides working and resting at his own pace, Independent Man enjoys his achievements fully. When the golden wheat stands ready for reaping, he can respond joyfully to its rippling beauty, knowing that his foresight and labor made the field fertile. When a new basket is woven, he can display it proudly to his wife and children, saying, "See what I made."

In industrial societies, few men ever know the pleasure of being able to say, "See what I made." One of the great paradoxes that impresses travelers is the contrast between the tense, suffering faces of the crowds in prosperous cities and the simple cheerfulness of some of the primitive peoples in "underdeveloped" nations. Given a modest amount of food and shelter, many a humble manual worker around the world derives more satisfaction from his daily work and goes home with lighter heart at sundown than affluent Americans who never pick up anything heavier than a telephone and live in luxurious comfort.

Independent Man works in a community of other persons whom he knows. (Never mind the possibility that he's fighting a blood feud with the Hatfields; this is theory.) When he mends a fence in bitter weather, he is encouraged not only by the fact that he is safeguarding his livestock but also by the protection he is giving his neighbor's crops. If some task is too much for him, he can count on that neighbor to help him with it. If he enjoys a little horse trading, he restrains any urge toward hyperbole he might have, because the other party is his friend. (And, being part of the community, the friend would have ample opportunity to get even.)

Independent Man is never a failure. He may be a clod at basket-weaving, plowing, or story-telling, but he is accepted in the community for whatever contributions he can make. His worth as a human being is not related to his performance in any particular occupation.

I have introduced Independent Man, not because I think many of him ever existed or that it would be possible to revive the type today, but only because the differences between his working life and ours are instructive. Although machinery has multiplied our productivity and freed us from the most back-breaking and dangerous kinds of labor, the accompanying reorganization of the structure of work has cost us much in freedom.

This process began with the earliest division of labor. The first worker was the Hunter. The food provider might have been hungry sometimes, but he was free. Today, food providers are not only a few hunters and farmers but also all the food processors, brokers, wholesalers, grocers, and other middlemen, including the workers who write the labels for the peanut butter jars. Instead of freedom, we have a tightly organized society in which 1 per cent of the employers hire 48 per cent of the workers.[1]

Working under direction is not necessarily a restriction of freedom. A majority of men no doubt would rather be led than undertake the responsibility of independent action or of leadership. But there should be a choice.

Some critics see today's occupational complex as a form of slavery. Because the only way to feel fulfilled in a utilitarian society is to perform "useful" tasks, we become chained to advancement in the big organizations that do utilitarian things in a big way. No whips keep us at our tasks, but it would be easier to overthrow a harsh tyrant than to rebel against ourselves. In accepting the prevalent values, we discard our freedom.

While maintaining political freedom in our country we have allowed many of our rights to be threatened by economic feudalism, complete with forced fealty. Most organizations expect their employees to avoid controversies which might reflect on the organization. And it is estimated that one-fifth of the labor force at present is covered by various loyalty programs.[2] Judging from Washington headlines of recent years, this means at least one worker out of five had better be a conformist or face the loss of his job whenever any intolerant group of superpatriots wants to make trouble for him.

Dissent won't get you the firing squad, but it can get you fired. Speaking of the dominant role of corporations as stewards of the continuing technological revolution, Supreme Court Justice William O. Douglas has asked, "To what extent have they become private governments . . . and repealed the Constitution?"[3]

The second worker was the Spear Maker, the provider of things. Today he works in manufacturing, distribution, or retailing. The joy of accomplishment once found in making a thing well has been lost. Nowadays, many jobs at which men who are adult citizens and heads of families are expected to work enthusiastically could be performed just as well by animals. Pigeons have been trained to inspect drug capsules and reject any that deviate from the standard. Experiments conducted by Dr. Marvin Grunzke of Holloman Air Force Base, New Mexico, show that chimpanzees could replace human workers in picking fruit or operating switchboards and punch presses. Chimps could also replace expensive analog computer equipment in chemical processing when the flow of reagents has to be varied to match the rate of reaction. (An Australian sheep rancher named Lindsay Schmidt has a rhesus monkey that performs the following chores: driving tractor, starting and stopping motor as necessary; picking burrs from sheep; herding sheep out of sheds after shearing; opening and shutting gates when sheep are moved from one field to another. Australian income tax authorities allow Schmidt to list the cost of the monkey's keep as a business expense deduction.)

Factory workers whose jobs have been fragmentized until they don't always know what contribution they're making to the finished product had better have a happy home life and diverting recreations. I have noticed that building tradesmen, who put up whole houses or finish plumbing jobs from start to flush, seem to be more cheerful than average. The Rev. Thomas M. Garrett, S.J., of the University of Scranton, an expert on business ethics, has observed:

> Interviews with businessmen and white collar workers unearth a profound discontent, a frustration, a feeling of guilt connected with their work. . . . Strangely enough, this dissatisfaction seems almost more common in the business and white collar class than among manual laborers and craftsmen.[4]

There is no substitute for the joy of achievement, which is now denied men even in creative fields. Goodman Ace, dean of comedy writers, makes this point about his profession. Any gag writer who can occasionally manage a funny thought on his way to the studio makes $1,000 a week. But, to hear Mr. Ace tell it, gag writers are a morose lot— badgered and belittled by comedians, producers, network executives, even the studio parking lot attendant. What hurts most is the absence of a sense of achievement. "If the rating [of the show] is high it reflects the talent of the comedian. When a show is in rating trouble a conference of the writers is called and, little by little . . . your lofty ideas will be whittled down to accommodate what is erroneously considered the level of mass consumption. Cryptic comments are rewritten into broad buffolas and scathing satire into euphemistic yaks."[5] In the gag-writing trade, continues Mr. Ace, the practitioners make jokes at tense moments about giving it all up and buying a candy store.

I recognize the mood. It is the same in advertising agencies. All copywriters periodically retire to a quiet corner of the office and brood about buying an interest in a small radio station. Newspapermen price country weeklies. The feeling usually comes over you after you have lost a battle with a committee.

The tribal Medicine Man was the precursor of all doctors, lawyers, and other professional men whose work satisfactions derive from directly and personally serving other men. Even in the old days, the Medicine Man charged a fee—a deerskin or a couple of mastodon steaks—but he meant well, and he made night calls. Today the success ethic undermines the traditional satisfactions of the professions. With everyone else scrambling toward materialistic goals, the professional man is persuaded to tighten up his bookkeeping. This makes him richer but not necessarily happier.

The higher status professions, says Dr. Esther Milner, social psychologist, "have come to exert a strong attraction for a certain kind of neurotic personality . . . persons with strong feelings of personal inadequacy."[6] Their long and costly training gives them an excuse for feeling that the world owes them a living. Thus, those who enter the professions with traditional idealism must collaborate and compete with individuals who are hell-bent to organize their field like the electrical equipment cartel—for profit.

Edward Bennett Williams, defender of such unpopular

personalities as James R. Hoffa and the late Senator Joseph McCarthy, has lamented that even law students are "rather blasé and unconcerned about some of the basic freedoms guaranteed by the Bill of Rights."[7] Williams regrets that a great many law students aspire to corporate or tax law, leaving the practice of criminal law to a small group of nonconformists. Although criminal law sometimes protects hoodlums who belong in jail, it also offers an inspiring challenge to those who hunger and thirst after justice. An innocent man with the power of the state against him needs a criminal lawyer of supreme skill.

Medicine Man, come back. I'll give you *two* deerskins.

The artists and scholars are descendants of the Cave-Wall Painter. To the extent that they remain true to their discipline they tend to escape the pressures I have mentioned. They are not without problems, however. Nowadays the artist may have a commercial sponsor and the scholar may be working on a government arms research program, which taints them after all with the same utilitarianism as everyone else. If they avoid exploitation, they have extreme difficulty making a living.

Last of the ancient tribe was the Chief, the manager, the man who sees the big picture. Ideally, he should have a fatherly love for his people, like the wise abbot described in the Rule of St. Benedict. There was a day when the virile Chief was in fact the father of his tribe; you can see how the idea began.

The Chief's role has changed, too. Relationships are no longer personal. Most Chiefs now are only Vice-Chiefs or Assistant Chiefs, with variously obstructed views of the big picture. They are unanimous, however, in holding that it is better to be any kind of Chief, no matter how low on the totem pole, than just another member of the tribe. They don't have much fun. Chiefs, in general, have little sense of humor.

Some medical authorities think the physical stresses of executive life have been exaggerated. The 250 corporation presidents who compose the presidents' panel of *Dun's Review* work an average of 60 to 70 hours a week, but they don't find their work load unduly burdensome because they set their own hours to a considerable extent.[8] Top executives have fewer heart attacks than their subordinates, according to a six-year study of 86,750 Du Pont employees.[9] The Du Pont medical director, Dr. Allen J. Fleming, said high blood pressure and ulcers, also stress-linked diseases, are no more common among executives than among ordinary workers.[10]

Although the myth of executive ill-health caused by tension seems to have been exploded, the subchiefs do suffer. "In my experience," says Dr. James M. MacMillan, medical director of the Reynolds Metal Co., "the most common single physical symptom of prolonged emotional distress in executives is the feeling of complete, chronic exhaustion. This exhaustion is present twenty-four hours a day and is unrelieved by rest or long hours of sleep."[11]

Emotional distress there is because, instead of achievement, the organizational in-fighting pays off in power. Dr. Stanley A. Rudin of Dalhousie University has concluded that the power motive is increasing in the United States. He based his conclusions on an analysis of popular literature and children's books.[12]

Power, as a reward for service to the organization, is

ephemeral. This helps explain why, in Dr. Milner's phrase, "for most older men in large urban settings, retirement takes from them their primary, in many instances, their sole source of their feelings of self-worth."[13]

When General Anthony C. McAuliffe, the man who said "Nuts" at Bastogne, was retired at sixty-five, according to company policy, as a vice-president and director of the American Cyanamid Co., he made an unusually frank statement to the press. Although he was planning a two-month trip to the Mediterranean with his wife, he said, "I'm already unhappy at the prospect of not coming to work tomorrow. I'm not going to like [retirement] unless I find something interesting to do."[14]

If these are the feelings of a man with a secure record of accomplishment, a widely known and respected military hero, what must be the sufferings of the ordinary corporation staffer when forced to retire! If a man's principal satisfaction in life was a certain power over a secretary and several assistants, what indeed is left when this is gone?

Those who never get to enjoy even a little power are still worse off. Denied gratification through work, men seek it in other ways, which may help explain a number of social problems. For instance, employees currently steal an estimated two billion dollars a year in money and merchandise from United States industry.[15] Sexuality is probably another outlet for frustration at work, with consequent stresses in family life and repercussions throughout society. The appalling rate of auto accidents is certainly related to the psychological climate of the work environment.

For more than half a century, traffic safety education

programs based on appeals to reason have failed to make noticeable impact. Even viewing horror films of traffic accidents fails to deter drivers from continuing their dangerous driving habits.[16] Advisory psychologists of the New York City traffic department are now studying the relationship between personality traits and accidents. The theory is that a motorist becomes angry at his wife or his employer, then projects his hostility toward any pedestrian or motorist who happens to cross his path.[17]

Religious leaders have often said that, while the rich may have trouble passing through the needle-narrow gate of Heaven, the poor cannot be expected to live virtuous lives if their poverty is extreme. The poverty of the Holy Family at Nazareth was ascetic simplicity. Destitution is dehumanizing and utterly evil.

Similarly, work can be both too easy and too hard for our spiritual welfare. As the great enterprise of every man's life, work molds him to its shape. Today, with so much work incapable in itself of yielding satisfaction, men must reach for power, prestige, and wealth in order to receive some return on the investment of the years of their lives. Otherwise, work can only be, as it is for a great many Americans, a burden to our spirits as well as our backs.

NOTES

1. C. Wright Mills, *White Collar*. New York: Oxford University Press, 1953.

2. R. S. Brown, Jr. *Loyalty and Security: Employment Tests in the United States*. New Haven: Yale University Press, 1958.

3. William O. Douglas, "Are Profits Profit Enough?" *The New York Times Book Review,* May 5, 1963.

4. *Ethics in Business.* New York: Sheed & Ward, 1963.

5. Goodman Ace, *The Book of Little Knowledge.* New York: Simon & Schuster, 1955.

6. Esther Milner, *The Failure of Success.* New York: Exposition Press, 1959.

7. *Arlington Heights (Ill.) Herald,* February 28, 1963.

8. *Chicago Daily News,* March 8, 1963.

9. *Chicago Daily News,* September 13, 1963.

10. *New York Times,* September 17, 1962.

11. *Chicago Daily News,* August 16, 1963.

12. *Science News Letter,* September 7, 1963.

13. Milner, *op. cit.*

14. *Chicago Daily News,* August 1, 1963.

15. *New York Times,* June 16, 1963.

16. *New York Times,* June 29, 1963.

17. *New York Times,* May 3, 1963.

5

What Kind of Job Is There in This Future?

I was having lunch with a friend who works for an advertising agency. It is customary on such occasions, as a humorous conversation-starter, for writers to indulge in self-pity. Without revealing any business secrets, each advances evidence that he has to contend with management, co-workers, clients, and products that are surely the world's greatest obstacles to advertising creativity. For once, my friend failed to greet me with two or three amusing anecdotes about his most recent frustrations.

"Either you have lost your spirit," I said, "or you have been promoted to such stratospheric heights of eminence that there's no one to complain about except yourself."

He explained his subdued mood. "The boss dropped by my office this morning, apparently just to chat. Every now and then he forgets to be predatory and acts human. That always disturbs me. As long as it's business as usual, I know how to protect my flanks. But when he acts human, I don't

know how to respond. I feel there should be some exchange of warmth; then I wonder if he's trying to trick me
in some subtle way I haven't figured out, and I pull back. I
wind up suspecting there's something wrong with me. If I
resent his being the boss, and I suppose I do, why can't
I forgive him for it?"

We agreed that the circumstances of a man's working
life inhibit the growth of meaningful relationships between
persons. The tensions of organizational competition are at
least as ancient as the bureaucracy of Egypt under the
Pharaohs. No doubt, the advisers of kings like Louis XIV
and Peter the Great had difficulty regarding each other as
brothers in Christ rather than obstacles to promotion.
Today, however, a much greater proportion of the population is caught up in competitive intrigues than was possible before the mechanization of agriculture.

In traditional Christian teaching, work is a bond between
persons, not a barrier. "Work itself is indeed love," writes
Stefan Cardinal Wyszynski, primate of Poland, "it is the
showing-forth, the witnessing, of love . . . Work is man's
tendency to draw near his fellow-man; it cannot aim at
emptiness. It always links us with people, if not immediately, then at least indirectly."[1]

Cardinal Wyszynski's book, *Work*, is a particularly
lucid statement of traditional teaching. Suppose Henry
Strively, typical young executive, has just read it (or heard
a good sermon by a priest who has read it). Like a man in
the first flush of good intentions after a weekend retreat, he
resolves to incorporate his work into his spiritual life.

On his way to his office the next morning, he greets the

receptionist as a person. Until then he had always treated her as a playback device for recorded fibs like "Mr. Strively can't see you now because he is in a meeting" or "Mr. Strively won't be back from the Australian branch office till a month from Tuesday." Startled by being looked at as another human being, she watches him suspiciously as he continues down the corridor.

"Watch out for Strively today," she remarks to a secretary. "Did you see him give me the eye?"

In the familiar surroundings of his office, Strively recalls that his work is supposed to link him with other men in the bond of love. Hector Gladly, that old pirate, is his brother in Christ and vice versa. If this thought has ever occurred to Gladly, he has shown no signs of it. The impersonality of the very atmosphere weighs heavily on Strively's spirits, and his resolutions of the night before begin to weaken.

Also his brother in Christ, like everyone else in the office, is that snake, Edgerton, who is in direct competition with him for the next promotion in their department. Strively considers his position. It is true that their competition has been conducted honorably, according to the commonly accepted rules. Edgerton, for instance, is unlikely to have made disparaging remarks about Strively behind his back. But each of them is fully resolved that in the long run the other will be his assistant, and to achieve that end tries to look and sound smarter and more efficient, turn out more work, show more enthusiasm, and please the management better.

With dismay, Strively sees that his new attitude has placed him at a disadvantage. A Christian does his job as well as possible, but it is most unloving of him to exult on those occasions when the excellence of his own work shows up a co-worker as the dolt that he is. Competition and Christianity are awkward in each other's presence.

Strively wonders how to go about using his job as a means of expressing love, not only for his income tax dependents, but also for Gladly, Edgerton, and the rest. In a rare flash of self-knowledge, he realizes that he may do fairly well at the virtue of justice, acting honorably toward Edgerton despite temptations to make trouble for him, but that to practice the virtue of charity toward Edgerton at the moment is beyond his strength.

Traditional Christian teaching on work turns out to include some of the famous hard sayings.

Just as Strively reaches this point in his interior dialog, a memo reaches his desk. It announces that Edgerton, having resigned to take a job with Interplanetary's chief competitor, will be replaced by a new man who will join the Interplanetary Corporation in three weeks. Strively is shocked. He had been beginning to get used to old Edgerton. The new man will be a complete stranger, one with whom Strively will have to build an entirely new relationship. A stranger who possibly will know a few tricks that Edgerton never heard of. Strively wishes he had Edgerton back; it might not be so hard to love Edgerton after all.

The Christian viewpoint overturned the attitude of the ancient world, which considered physical work demeaning, an activity for slaves. Christ himself was a manual worker, as were most of the Apostles and first disciples. The New Testament abounds in illustrations and comparisons from the lives of artisans and farmers. Contrary to the idea that work is a sad necessity for those who can't get out of it, Christianity preached that work is a means of perfecting man's nature.

"Even before his fall man had to work. For he had to dress paradise ... It is not, then, the result of original sin," says Cardinal Wyszynski. "Only afterwards sin added oppressiveness, hardship, sweat and weariness to work, which was always man's duty."[2]

Man cannot desire complete liberation from the hardships of work because these very hardships, endured in the proper spirit, are the means of freeing him from sin. "Work, by its difficulty, redeems, liberates, ennobles and sanctifies."[3]

In joining our work to the work of those who have labored before us and those who will take up our tasks when we are gone, we participate in a special communion of saints. Work must be performed for love of God in order to be truly salutary. Work for personal enrichment or the glory of the state scores no supernatural points, no matter how energetic or heroic. It is not possible, in the Cardinal's opinion, "to do lasting, versatile, fruitful, effective work without linking it with prayer."[4]

He concedes that this is not easy, because prayer draws us away from the world while work pulls us towards it. The link can be strengthened if we remain aware that we work always in God's presence and offer our work to Him, in the words of the Mass:

"We offer thee, O Lord, the chalice of salvation. . . ."

Cardinal Wyszynski takes pains to reject those claims advanced for work which arise from the materialism common to Marxist societies and our own. Utilitarianism re-

gards contemplation as a waste of time. Everyone must
work, in a productive, tangible sense, or be considered a
parasite. This manner of thinking overemphasizes the importance of work.

> Man is lost in the pursuit of profit, driven 'by duty,'
> which he often understands rather as a sense of ex-
> ternal need than as a moral value. . . . We are so
> absorbed in and engrossed by the perfecting of what
> we do that we completely forget about ourselves. We
> even consider that excess of work frees us from the
> duty of moulding our own souls.[5]

Individuals who take a balanced attitude toward work
suffer. Depending on where they live, they see themselves
losing ground to Stakhanovites or company men. The Cardinal defends feasts and holidays as a means of deliverance
from an excess of work and insists that men should have
energies left over from their work to remain social beings,
because "it is very easy for over-worked people to become
materialists."[6] When work becomes more of an end than a
means, you can't tell the bureaucrats of a socialist state
from capitalist executives with a briefcase full of work for
the weekend.

In the industrially advanced countries, few workers are
dehumanized by physical burdens beyond human endurance. But there is no doubt that the climate of the work
environment often has a coarsening effect on human sensi-
bilities instead of ennobling the human personality as it
should.

I have summarized Cardinal Wyszynski's ideas on work

at some length because their context attaches a special significance to the restatement of traditional teaching. He wrote mainly for his flock in Poland, where a Communist regime is attempting to impose its Marxist views on a Christian population. In hard-working Poland, still recovering from the devastation of World War II, he warns his people against "longing for those future happy times when work will show itself to be superfluous."[7] Such longings are unworthy because of the supernatural values attainable through work, which he explains in detail.

In the United States, however, the problem of superfluous work is no longer theoretical. For better or worse, the fruits of automation are falling on our heads like Newton's mythical apple. John I. Snyder, Jr., chairman of U.S. Industries, Inc., manufacturers of automation equipment, testified before a Senate Labor subcommittee that automation is eliminating 40,000 jobs a week. Subsequently, he stated that this estimate may be too low.[8] He ridiculed the common belief that new jobs created by automation, such as manufacturing and maintaining the equipment, can help take up the slack.

Secretary of Labor W. Willard Wirtz says the new machines have, on the average, ability comparable to that of a high school graduate. Since, at the current school dropout rate, more than a third of the 26 million new workers who will enter the labor market in the next decade will not have finished high school, the machines will offer more advantages to their users than ever.[9]

It is estimated that one-third of the jobs being automated out of existence are white collar jobs.[10] Computers are taking over the clerical work of airlines, banks, insurance companies, even government agencies (despite the fact that machines can't vote). One $24 million airline installation reserves tickets and hotel rooms, handles cargo billing and lading, maps flight plans, keeps track of spare engine parts, does market and route research, and will be able to handle supersonic flight problems when the time comes. Eighty per cent of all the bank checks written in America are already processed by computers. In the brokerage business, 10,000 clerks have been eliminated in two years. Oddly enough, the computers tend to eliminate the higher level clerical jobs first.

The machines are threatening middle management, too. Martin-Marietta selects scientists and engineers to work on new space contracts, not with a platoon of personnel men, but with a computer. A Chicago advertising agency dispensed with ten media executives when computers demonstrated they could do a better job of selecting time spots for television commercials. In England, the British National Coal Board began to operate at a profit when many management duties were turned over to computers.

At a conference of automation experts in Boston, Thomas L. Whistler, associate professor of industrial relations at the University of Chicago graduate business administration school, described a plan for automating regional steel distribution warehouses. The computers could analyze past demand patterns, mill output, costs, and other factors, then make more accurate decisions on inventory control problems than human managers could. In the long run, he predicted, one manager will be able to operate several warehouses, leaving several executives jobless.[11]

Not even the professions are safe from electronic competition. A Univac "law clerk" has been demonstrated that checks 120,000 legal references a minute. Within 24 hours, it can provide a lawyer with full information on prior cases and decisions relating to a particular subject—work that would take a lawyer a week or more to complete in a law library.

Early in 1964 a group of economists, publishers, educators, labor leaders and other experts, calling themselves the Ad Hoc Committee on the Triple Revolution, addressed a much-discussed memorandum to President Johnson which related the cybernetics revolution to the nuclear weapon revolution and the world-wide human rights revolution. As it becomes increasingly apparent to various governments (one hopes) that war is impossible, the 10 per cent of our gross national product devoted to military and space projects is likely to decrease, resulting in further loss of jobs. Regarding the third revolution the memorandum said:

> The demand of the civil rights movement cannot be fulfilled within the present context of society. The Negro is trying to enter a social community and a tradition of work-and-income which are in the process of vanishing even for the hitherto privileged white workers.[12]

One of the signers of the memorandum, Robert Theobald, consulting economist for the United Nations, believes

that full employment has become an impossible goal. He
suggests as the only possible alternative to mass unemployment, poverty, and despair an "absolute, constitutional
right" to an income for everyone, whether he has a job or
not.[13]

Income without work is a new idea only with respect to
the poorer members of society. More than one-fifth of the
personal income of Americans now comes from sources
other than jobs, such as dividends, interest, rents, life insurance payments, private pension funds, Social Security, and
other state and federal payments of various kinds. Sylvia
Porter, syndicated columnist, says persons enjoying this
type of income have tripled since 1949 and increased by
one-third since 1958. There are now 7.3 million of them, of
whom two million are less than sixty-five years old.[14]

Michael D. Reagan, Syracuse University political scientist and another member of the Ad Hoc Committee, argues
that it is feasible to guarantee every family in the nation an
income of at least $3,000, which would greatly benefit 9.3
million families whose present incomes average only $1,795.

> What would it cost? A detailed answer cannot be
> given at this point, yet we have one related estimate
> that is worth considering. The President's Council of
> Economic Advisers says that about $11 billion a year
> would bring all poor families up to the $3,000 income
> level. . . . The burden—one-fifth of the annual de-
> fense budget, less than two per cent of gross national
> product—would certainly not be intolerable.[15]

Dr. Yale Brozen, professor of business economics at the University of Chicago, is an optimistic prophet.

The common man will become a university-educated world traveler with a summer place in the country, enjoying such leisure time activities as sailing and concert-going; able to call on superior medical services to maintain his health, eating exotic foods from the far corners of the world in fine restaurants, and living in a home equipped with beautiful furniture and paintings.[16]

Buckminster Fuller, whose inventive mind gives his opinions weight, foresees that "we can make life on earth a general success for all men instead of assuming negatively that success and even prolonged survival" are for a fortunate few. For Fuller, the problem of the future is not how we shall make our livings but how we can organize an educational system to serve the entire population in a relatively workless world.[17]

The Ad Hoc Committee on the Triple Revolution concluded that with any luck automation will proffer

an existence qualitatively richer in democratic as well as material values. A social order in which men make the decisions that shape their lives becomes more possible now than ever before; the unshackling of men from the bonds of unfulfilling labor frees them to become citizens, to make themselves and to make their own history.[18]

The Christian response to such prospects is to rejoice, not because unworthy desires may be fulfilled, but because amid abundance a more humane view of the good life may prevail. Some businessmen expect a decline of interest in consumer products. Nelson N. Foote, an executive of the General Electric Co., has said: "The consumer in the year 2000 may devote his attention mainly to the satisfaction of wants that do not require consumption, or production, or distribution, like stimulating conversation."[19]

Many of the exhibits at the New York World's Fair portray the future in terms of a surfeit of consumer goods, which may be one reason the Fair has been widely criticized for lacking the prophetic vision of great expositions of the past. The sensitive visitor to the Fair felt that even in 1964 the gadgety emphasis may have been slightly behind the times.

A difficult period of adjustment to radical changes in daily life undoubtedly lies ahead. Suppose a way is found to guarantee a living to everyone? The pleasanter kinds of work like directing important enterprises, controlling machinery that's exciting to operate, and exercising unusual skills will be sought after in fierce competition, while in order to fill the less appealing jobs society will have to provide greatly improved working conditions and attractive emoluments. Individuals with marginal abilities will be paid cheerfully to stay home out of the way.

This doesn't promise withering away of the competitive spirit in favor of the growth of love, but there is reason to hope for a friendlier climate for the Christian worker than Henry Strively is used to.

With a guaranteed minimum income some men will

choose to loaf through life. Others—artists, writers, actors, poets, students—can use a modest degree of economic freedom as the base for an upsurge of creativity similar to that of classical Greece. A number of scholars are excited about this possibility, pointing out a parallel between the human slaves who provided Aristotle with leisure and the automatic slaves we are acquiring to provide similar leisure for all men capable of taking advantage of it.

In the new Golden Age we can expect increased popular interest in community affairs, politics, the arts, philosophy, religious contemplation and the nuances of personal relationships. New religious orders may arise to deal with new needs, one to dedicate itself to unattractive but necessary jobs that can't be automated, another to provide spiritual direction for a new kind of layman who has more interest in religion and more time to pursue it.

Gerard Piel, publisher of *Scientific American* and a member of the Ad Hoc Committee on the Triple Revolution, has observed that already

the greatest feats of human capacity in our society are performed for incentives other than the material ones —the work of our scientists, the work of a first-rate physician in a teaching hospital. These are glorious achievements of the human spirit that are not motivated by material gain but by the work itself and its inherent rewards.

With the traditional job-income relationship losing its force, Piel expects economic competition to decline also.

I think we could sum up the difference between (this) side of the watershed in human history. . . . and the side that we are moving into in the following terms: In the society of scarcity, one man's well-being could be increased only at the expense of the other man's well-being. It is plain that the society of abundance presents us with entirely the opposite situation, in which one man's well-being can be increased only through the increase in the well-being of all others.[20]

Where does all this leave Henry Strively, poised here and now between the call of his higher nature and the cost of higher education for his children? There is never a pat answer to a moral dilemma. However, attitudes toward work could be changing faster than anyone realizes, to Strively's benefit. We live at a time when predicting the speed of change is riskier than predicting the speed of racehorses.

Even so, it is obviously a good deal too soon for the Strivelys of the world to expose themselves freely to the mercies of the Gladlys and the Edgertons. "Starry-eyed idealism must be tempered by hard-headed practicality, which sees that ideals are attainable only in terms of existing institutional structures," says the Rev. Thomas M. Garrett, S.J., in his study of business ethics.

The man of good-will cannot as a rule transform the business world without power, status, and income. These are, and always will be, important tools. Anyone who despises them is living apart from the mainstream of modern life; only those who control these three forces will be able to change the business world and the conditions of work.[21]

Henry Strively must learn to know himself well enough to distinguish between simple defeatism and Christian resignation, without abandoning the world to those who lack his scruples. A delicate task. If he is a failure at the office, he is a double failure. If he succeeds at the office, he probably pays the price of failure in some other area of his life.

As I keep telling you, failure is an important subject.

NOTES

1. *Work.* Chicago: Scepter, 1960.
2. *Ibid.*
3. *Ibid.*
4. *Ibid.*
5. *Ibid.*
6. *Ibid.*
7. *Ibid.*
8. *Chicago Daily News*, December 2, 1963.
9. *Chicago Daily News*, December 2, 1963.
10. Thomas O'Toole, "White-Collar Automation," *The Reporter*, December 5, 1963.
11. *New York Times*, October 30, 1962.
12. Text published in *Advertising Age*, April 6, 1964.
13. *Chicago Daily News*, September 21, 1963.
14. *Chicago Daily News*, December 11, 1963.
15. Michael D. Reagan, "For a Guaranteed Income," *New York Times Magazine*, June 7, 1964.

16. *Science News Letter,* November 30, 1963.
17. *New York Times,* September 13, 1963.
18. *Op. cit.*
19. *Advertising Age,* November 18, 1963.
20. *Catholic Reporter,* June 19, 1964.
21. *Ethics in Business.* New York: Sheed & Ward, 1963.

6

Failure by Moonlight

All work and no play make Jack a typical American. Contrary to the general impression that we are living in a golden age of widespread leisure, research argues convincingly that we are nearly all "moonlighters" at heart. This is documented in a three year study sponsored by the Twentieth Century Fund.[1] Among other surprises, it shows that we still work as hard or perhaps harder than did the serfs of the Middle Ages.

Americans have been feeling good about government figures indicating that the average work week has decreased from 69.7 hours in 1850 to 38.5 hours. That looks like an increase of more than 31 hours of free time every week. Many of us wonder how our personal lives can be so badly arranged that we don't seem to have as much free time as our grandparents had. Years ago, when the work week was supposed to be 60 to 70 hours folks spent summer evenings sitting out on the front porches that were a feature of the residential architecture of the times. Now most of those front porches are gone. We use their replacement, the patio, for entertaining but never have time to go out there and just sit. Our conversations frequently refer to the "rat race" and the "treadmill."

The Twentieth Century Fund report, written by Sebastian de Grazia, a political scientist and philosopher, explains why the apparent increase in free time is mostly an illusion. During the Middle Ages, for example, the 52 Sundays, added to something like 115 holidays in most places, made 167 holidays a year. These holidays were observed by the lower classes of society as well as the nobility. This translates to an average work week of about 45.6 hours.

The gain in free time since 1850 also disappears under scrutiny. Consider the history of a mythical family, the Drudges. Old Elijah Drudge averaged 65.7 hours at the mill in 1850 (not 69.7—that figure reflects the longer hours of farm workers). But he didn't fling himself at the job with the concentration expected of modern workers. Efficiency experts, production lines, and time clocks hadn't been invented yet. Elijah set his own pace and looked out the window when he felt like it. After work he walked home in only a few minutes. Commuting was no problem to anyone. In 1850, 85 per cent of the population of the United States lived in places with fewer than 2,500 inhabitants.

Elijah Drudge was no do-it-yourselfer, either. Like most breadwinners in 1850, he rented his house. Repairs, which were inexpensive, were the landlord's responsibility. Even if Elijah had enjoyed puttering, he couldn't have done much. There were no power tools. Materials did not come cut to size, prefinished and otherwise designed especially to assist home handymen of no great skill.

Nor did Elijah have to go to the supermarket. His wife Hannah strolled a few blocks to the store when convenient. Otherwise, she sent one of the children with a note, and the grocer's boy would deliver everything she needed. Hannah never asked Elijah to help with the housework. Family units were larger then. Although there was more housework to do, there were usually female relatives around to help. Hannah's widowed aunt, who lived with them, was the kind that scrubbed the door step every day.

In the present generation, the descendants of Elijah and Hannah Drudge include two distant cousins, Mike Drudge, a skilled factory worker, and John P. Drudge, a young executive. Mike works 45.2 hours a week, the national average in 1960 for full time industrial workers (and no looking out the window). Like an estimated 11 per cent of the labor force, Mike averages an hour a week at a second job. He spends eight and a half hours a week commuting. Another five hours a week go for do-it-yourselfing around the house. (According to the 1960 census, home owners now outnumber renters by a ratio of three to two.) If Mike lived in an apartment instead of his own house, he'd still probably have to do some decorating and other work. In addition, he uses up two hours a week helping his wife with housework and shopping. (These figures are all averages.)

Totaling it all up gives Mike a work week that allows only about four hours more free time than Elijah Drudge enjoyed in 1850. The comparison can't be made exact. For instance, Mike now gets a paid vacation every year, which adds free time. But there are many factors not yet mentioned that take it away. One-fifth of American families now move in any given year, usually for reasons associated with work. Preparation for moving and recovery afterwards involve countless hours. And, in an increasingly technological age, many workers have work-connected reading to do at home.

John P. Drudge's life is much like Mike's in the expenditure of time for activities like commuting, do-it-yourselfing, housework, and shopping. His "moonlighting" is done on one job, since he works the typical executive week of 55 hours. What's wrong here? Mike, the factory worker, has a shorter work week than John, the executive. In the nineteenth century, when England was the mercantile center of the world, London executives of any stature took four-day weekends. It might be expected that business management would reward itself with more free time as well as good incomes. But no. Americans in the twentieth century are so obsessed with work that they choose to work longer hours whenever the choice is theirs.

Workers like Mike choose to "moonlight." Executives like John have made an institution of the barbarous habit of the business lunch and not infrequently work as long as 70 hours a week. Two-thirds of them regularly bring home work to do nights and weekends. Asked what they would do if suddenly given an independent income, 90 per cent of a sampling of executives said they would continue working at their jobs. For an executive to declare that he needed more time for serious reading and thinking, being therefore unable to read all the interoffice memos over the weekend, would be felt as a stab at the heart of the free enterprise system.

Housewives commonly retire from business with the birth of their first child and spend several exceedingly busy years thereafter. Then a day comes when the children need less care. With modern appliances and services, the woman begins to have considerable free time. So what does she do? She gets a job.

In 1890 only 18 per cent of females over the age of 14 had jobs. Today the percentage is double that. Six out of every ten women working are married and their average age is over forty.

What about retirement, the "golden years?"

Most men have not been conditioned to enjoy retiring at age sixty or sixty-five. Those in moderately good health are forced to retire by company policy or they would stay on the job to the end.

Surely, those few Americans who are independently wealthy must be exceptions to this preoccupation with work. A millionaire doesn't need a pay check. But the fact is that they work like everyone else. Except for an extremely small group of cafe society playboys, all America's rich men are busy as bankers, lawyers, executives, or politicians, doing something productive.

Not only do we Americans work virtually as long as we ever did, we don't seem to want it any other way. Some critics say that after working as long as we can manage we misuse the free time left because we feel that we should still be working. We have become so infected with utilitarianism that we can't enjoy anything unless we can persuade

ourselves it is somehow useful. If an American strolls in a
beautiful park, attends a concert or play, he tells himself he
is recharging his batteries to have another go at climbing the
business pyramid.

As recently as the eighteenth century, men still understood "leisure" in the same sense as classical Greece. When
labor leaders, public officials, and others use the term "more
leisure time" in discussing the theoretically shorter work
week, they mean something quite different. Hardly anyone
in this country today enjoys true leisure.

Instead of "leisure," we should say "free time," that time
which is not spent working, commuting, or doing chores.
True leisure is the state of being free of necessity to work,
in order to do something worth doing for its own sake. A
man at leisure can be lying in a hammock thinking or
strenuously sculpturing a figure in granite. The sculpturing
is not work because work is something one does to earn a
living and which one would not do without pay or some
other motive not related to the work itself. (A woman's
housework can be a mixture. Floor scrubbing is clearly
work. Cooking can be creative.)

Despite the considerable length of the actual work week,
many Americans enjoy a reasonable amount of free time.
Only 13 per cent admit to having no hobbies or favorite
recreations. The industries built by the demand for recrea-
tional materials and services are thriving. But recreation is
not leisure. Recreation is an activity that rests us after work
and restores our energies for more work.

The absence of true leisure in our society handicaps the
growth of great ideas. Most of mankind's finest moments in
science, philosophy, art, politics, and religion have been the

fruit of someone's leisure. Without leisure, there can be feverish activity and much apparent progress in details, but little originality. De Grazia says that even on the campuses of universities, where the idea of leisure would be expected to be understood and cherished, there are only work, free time, and recreation.

The contemporary rage for research (as opposed to simple study), the projects embarked on (requiring 'teamwork' research), the increase in school bureaucracy, of machine and paper work—practices as yet foreign to European universities—insure that leisure sets no foot on campus.[2]

Jacques Barzun, dean of Columbia University, is so certain that campuses are without leisure that he has predicted the end of the liberal arts tradition in American higher education. He said the atmosphere on campus today is one of "anxious preoccupation." Both teachers and students "are impatient with everything that is not directed at the development of talent into competence." In contrast to the ivy-covered image of the college as a place where scholars leisurely ponder ideas, "students are married, employed, going to or returning from a conference, apprehensive about examinations, ruled by the clock like the most harried executive."[3]

Another critic who agrees that Americans have lost their understanding of leisure is the Rev. William McNamara, O.C.D., director of the new Spiritual Life Institute. He says:

We have a compulsive desire to work not because of greed or materialism, which is what our enemies and our moralists accuse us of, but because of a philosophy that we inherited and still cherish: namely that value depends entirely upon utility, (that) only useful activity is valuable, meaningful, moral.[4]

Consequently, we do not know how to contemplate, although "everything that we can bear witness to concerning the reality of God derives from contemplation." Father McNamara's Spiritual Life Institute is working on a program through which some Americans may find their way back to contemplation. The idea is to provide special houses in which both religious and lay men and women may live for a time—at leisure.

Father McNamara recalls a saying of St. John of the Cross: "Those who rush headlong into good works without having acquired through contemplation the power to act will accomplish little more than nothing, and sometimes nothing at all, and sometimes even harm."

He adds: "What is true of good works is true, even more so, of merely worldly activity."[5]

De Grazia distinguishes between ordinary people and the "leisure kind." Most people use the money earned by work to buy various pleasures for themselves and their families in their free time. Their work can be of the most necessary and ennobling type. Their recreations can be admirable. They have no reason to be apologetic about not being the leisure kind. And they are wise to avoid sloth and idleness.

The leisure kind are those who love ideas and the play of

the imagination. "In one century they may be scientists, in another theologians, in some other bards, whatever the category may be that grants them the freedom to let their minds play. They invent the stories, they create the cosmos, they discover what truth it is given man to discover." The leisure kind may "work, steal, flirt, fight, like all the others," but their attitude towards work and time is entirely different from that of the majority of humanity.[6]

Distinctions between work and recreation or free time do not exist for the leisure kind who are in a state of leisure —that is, free of necessity. To distinguish a philosopher from a hobo at first glance might be difficult. Many of the great figures upon whose use of leisure civilization has been built would be jailed for vagrancy today in most American towns. The leisure kind embrace an activity for its own sake, not because it is useful, or well-paying, or looked up to by others.

Leisure can be achieved two ways. Washington, Jefferson, Madison, and most of the other Founding Fathers of the nation had the leisure to think about politics and create a brilliant new system because they were prosperous landowners. Aristocracies can be highly creative. A long line of starving-in-a-garret artists and thinkers also have achieved leisure, by cutting their needs to the minimum. Thoreau said, "My greatest skill has been to want but little."

The Drudge family has another descendant in the twentieth century who happens to be the leisure kind. He is Pearson Drudge-Knott, the poet. Drudge-Knott encountered much better fortune than the leisure kind can generally expect these days. While he was a college student, his talent for poetry was recognized and encouraged, but he married one of his classmates soon after graduation. As head of a family he had to take a job writing continuity for a small-town radio station. He managed to write a little poetry evenings and weekends. At the end of five years he had published half a dozen poems in obscure magazines and worked up to a better job with a television station.

Then his wife inherited a farm on the outskirts of a rapidly growing suburb. As a farm it had provided only a small income for the old folks, but when it was sold to real-estate developers the land fetched nearly a quarter of a million dollars. Drudge-Knott resigned from the television station the next day. With their children's education assured by this sudden wealth, Drudge-Knott and his wife now live modestly on the interest. He devotes his full time at home to writing poetry and literary criticism.

Drudge-Knott adheres to a rigid daily schedule. From breakfast until one o'clock he writes. After lunch, he attends to correspondence, household chores, and research until four o'clock. From four to five, he meditates. The dinner hour and early evening he spends with the family. Then there is time for a couple of hours of reading and study before bedtime.

Occasionally, the Drudge-Knotts engage in the same pleasures as other people—entertaining friends, going to shows or concerts, enjoying various sports and outings. He prefers that his writing schedule be disturbed only rarely. Superficially, his single-mindedness resembles that of some business executives. One difference is that Drudge-Knott goes for months without doing anything more useful in the utilitarian sense than changing the light bulb in his study.

The quiet routine of an undisturbed poet or paleontologist would give the non-leisure kind a frothing fit in less than six weeks. They'd rather work a double shift in a sweat shop.

It must be admitted that if society consisted entirely of the leisure kind we could scarcely expect much economic expansion. De Grazia observes that Socrates' whole life had no effect whatever on the Gross National Product of his day "except perhaps for the government's expense at the time of his trial."[7] There are places in the world today where the villagers would walk in the mud all their lives without building a sidewalk unless someone from outside talked them into it. They could use more of the utilitarian spirit.

Americans have plenty of it available for export. Here, men who would be the leisure kind in another time and place become persuaded that they should be go-getters. Their frustrations are epic. And those who are not the leisure kind are denied the moments of peace and introspection that everyone needs.

No one knows what will happen in the future as automation continues to give millions plenty of free time whether they like it or not. Unfortunately, there is reason to believe many of us will be failures at leisure, too.

NOTES

1. Sebastian de Grazia, *Of Time, Work and Leisure*. New York: Twentieth Century Fund, 1962.

2. *Ibid.*

3. *New York Times*, December 12, 1963.

4. *The Catholic Reporter*, October 26, 1962.

5. *Ibid.*

6. De Grazia, *op. cit.*

7. *Ibid.*

7

Termites in the Mahogany

While browsing through the business books at the library, I noticed a new title on the self-help shelf that amused me: *How to Achieve Success and Happiness in Business.* A few years ago I don't think the words "and happiness" would have been included. Achieving "success" would have been enough. A successful man was assumed to be happy; if he wasn't, he should see a psychiatrist.

Until recently, we esteemed human activities in direct proportion to their payoff in titles, income, and mahogany-paneled offices. We thought almost any kind of success better than any kind of failure.

When a racketeer whose mouthpiece had managed to keep him out of jail, but just barely, drove around in his Day-Glo pink Jaguar, he attracted admiring and envious glances even from some who knew how he made his money. At the same time, honest men handicapped in the competitive struggle by their integrity had to endure the sneers of their in-laws for not being more successful.

It is difficult for most men to be detached about success. Having attached so much importance for so long to utilitarian activity, the middle-class male can maintain his self-respect only through occupational achievement. To fail occupationally, losing out on a key promotion or being fired for inadequate performance, is to fail as a person, a loss of face too bitter to bear. Male suicide rates in the United States parallel the prevalence of unemployment. Some researchers believe unemployment "may be the main cause of suicide."[1]

Many individuals still pursue the success ethic uncritically, which discourages, among others, Dr. J. L. Zwingle, vice president of Cornell University. Young people, he said, "catch on pretty fast to what society rewards—in our age it is professional success. For example, what happens if a chap wants to become a musician, an artist? They'll say he can't make a living that way."[2]

But if you look closely enough you can find evidence of a growing change of mood. The success ethic is being questioned. I don't mean the complaints heard for years by bartenders in cocktail lounges where martinis cost a buck. This is new. Louder and louder criticism from moralists is accompanied by a foot-shuffling, shifty-eyed attitude among those who once seemed imperviously complacent.

Traditional routes to success are losing the appeal they used to hold for energetic youth. The salesman, for instance, has always enjoyed opportunity plus expenses. In most companies, while everyone else is spending money full-time, only the salesmen are regarded as bringing money in. Despite the favored treatment which management extends to salesmen because of this circumstance, a recent survey of sixty large firms showed that recruiting new salesmen is the biggest problem of sales managers. College graduates in particular are reluctant to become salesmen.[3]

Advertising, a closely related field in which the plums also ripen fairly close to the ground, has lost its glamor, too. In a survey of high school boys, only 7.8 per cent thought a career in advertising would be exciting, and half didn't think it could be even moderately interesting.[4]

Possibly, these changing attitudes are related to public indignation about such episodes as the almost simultaneous exposure of illegal price-fixing in three industries, electrical manufacturing, steel forgings, and copper and brass tubing. The spectacle of executives from long-established and conservative firms going to jail contributes to the unsettled spirit of the age. When a suburban church polled its members on their preference in topics for sermons, their first choice was "serenity." Also high on the list were requests for "How to be a Christian in the Business World."[5]

Dr. Robert E. Fitch, dean of the Pacific School of Religion, when interviewed by the Center for the Study of Democratic Institutions, suggested an explanation:

> The American people have lost three or four idols—Baalim—in the last decade or two. One is the belief in Mammon, in the power of wealth to do everything. We have lost our faith in that because even though we are now a wealthy country, very affluent, it does not solve all our problems.[6]

Dr. Esther Milner, University of Alberta social psychologist, has observed:

The reaction of today's more sensitive, gifted and emotionally hardy teen-agers and young adults against the obsessive materialism and inner denial of the times in which they are growing up cannot be overlooked as a major hope for the future.[7]

Rejection of Mammon takes various forms. There is, for instance, the niece of Hector Gladly's wife. A beatnik. A misfortune of which Gladly never speaks, especially within hearing of his executive colleagues at Interplanetary Corporation. The niece grew up in a small town in Georgia, where her father operated a garage. He believed wholeheartedly in the success ethic, in which faith he was confirmed every winter as Yankee tourists bound for Florida gave him the opportunity to increase his capital by making emergency repairs at inflated prices. An intelligent, sensitive girl, the garageman's daughter rejected her life in Georgia, with its crude greed, provincialism, and intellectual unawareness. She was disturbed also because socially, even in Nowheresville, she was nobody.

Moving to New York City, she found a life much more to her liking. She slept, cooked, and lived on the floor of a former warehouse with other beatniks. Part-time work a few hours a week provided all the money she needed. While all the squares from her high school graduating class were selling dry goods or filing accounts receivable back in Nowheresville, she was sleeping late at the pad or improvising *haiku* verses in the inspirational environment of the Museum of Modern Art.

The warehouse was frequently loud with heated conversation about the arts. Several of the residents were talented;

all were interested. Everyone agreed that being an artist was a state of mind, a pattern of life. It was merely a fortunate circumstance if you had talent besides.

To Gladly's niece, a delightful fringe benefit of life on the fringe in the warehouse was that everybody was nobody. Which, of course, is another way of saying that everybody was somebody. When the city authorities decided that camping in warehouses and lofts was illegal, she was put out in more ways than one.

Another mode of escape from the success ethic is to go back to the land. A family somehow able to acquire the considerable capital now needed to live on a farm can isolate itself from the quiet desperation of urban life. "Isolate" is the correct word because you have to move so far out in the country that even the awning salesmen won't be able to find you. If you don't go far enough, you'll be surrounded within five years by real estate developments.

Once on the land, you can raise your own food organically, bake whole wheat bread, run for the legislature or at least the township board without bucking a big machine, and do many things for yourself which urban people spend extravagantly to have done for them. Although the joys of bucolic life are magnified in the minds of those who have never lived on a farm, they do exist. Especially for those who, because of wise investments in the stock market, can afford to farm with picturesque "family farm" methods.

Genuine farmers, who have to depend on the farm for all their income, can be as caught up in the success ethic as anyone.

Some critics of the success ethic believe more in action

than escape. Applications to join the Peace Corps are now
coming in at the rate of 40,000 a year. In terms of conventional success, serving in the Peace Corps, the Inter-Ameri-
can Co-operative Institute, the Papal Volunteers for Latin
America or any of the other proliferating organizations of
this type is a waste of time. There's no money in it. More
significantly, it does nothing to advance the individual in a
career.

The Peace Corps, assisted by ample press coverage, has
projected an accurate image of the sacrifices required of
volunteers. There can be few applicants who think they're
headed for titillating adventures in a tropical paradise
somewhere.

In the beginning, pessimists questioned whether Americans could be interested in hard work in poverty-stricken
villages, without plumbing, appliances, or familiar food.
No refrigerator, no beer to put in it, except perhaps some
local product that makes the absence of the real stuff all the
more poignant.

"Were Americans hardy enough to serve in remote
places, lacking many of the conveniences they had always
enjoyed? Would they work where malaria, yellow fever,
cholera, and dysentery were enemies?" Sargent Shriver,
Peace Corps director, was cheered by the answer. "We
soon learned that our volunteers were more than tough
enough, that the complaints about physical hardship were
insignificant . . . Americans are willing, even eager, to give
up the deadening comforts of a too easy affluence."[8]

There's no way of knowing how many individuals are
quietly making anti-success decisions late at night after

long conversations over coffee with their wives, decisions that will cost them thousands of dollars over the years, without attracting the attention of anyone but their creditors. Occasionally, you do hear of examples. I read recently about an Omaha advertising agency president who resigned to devote full time, without pay, to helping raise funds for a missionary school for Indian children in South Dakota. Clarence B. Randall, retired chief of Inland Steel and Presidential advisor, tells of an idealistic government worker earning about $14,000 a year "who was offered the presidency of a corporation with a salary of $50,000 if he would leave the government. He was occupying a post of great sensitivity at the time and felt that duty to his country had to be the controlling motive in his life."[9]

Thousands of dedicated persons still become priests, ministers, missionaries, nuns, or teachers for the traditional selfless reasons. They are outside this discussion because they haven't rejected success so much as ignored it. Passing up the peanuts entirely is not the same as eating a few and then putting down the bowl. For most men, the problem is not how to reject success, or ignore it, but how to nibble at it without making a pig of yourself.

Among those intensely involved in business, questions are being asked that would not have been raised ten years ago. The mere existence of a book like *The Business Conscience* by the Secretary of the Department of Commerce, Luther H. Hodges, is evidence of change. Mr. Hodges has seen a gradual but steady improvement in business ethics over the years. Practices once common have become unthinkable except among marginal operators. "The plain

fact is that the public expects more of today's businessmen
—and it receives more from them," he says.[10]

Mr. Hodges does not pretend that American business
suddenly has become a branch of the St. Vincent de Paul
Society. It worries him that businessmen aren't more concerned about ethics than they seem to be. However, he
knows many businessmen in important positions who are
not buying success-at-any-price.

The Rt. Rev. Msgr. George G. Higgins, director of the
National Catholic Welfare Conference social action department, reports Catholic interest in business ethics is developing at an "unexpectedly rapid rate." After listing a
number of new books and articles on the subject, he predicted in his weekly newspaper column:

> Perhaps the day will come, in the not too distant
> future, when Catholic, Protestant and Jewish experts
> in the field of business ethics will be able to meet—
> together with businessmen from their respective
> groups—in a joint conference similar to the extraordi-
> narily successful interfaith meeting which was held on
> the subject of race relations.[11]

Through surveys and interviews with business leaders,
the Rev. Raymond C. Baumhart, S.J., of Loyola University, Chicago, has become particularly well informed about
what businessmen think of business ethics. "In your industry, are there any generally accepted business practices
which you regard as unethical?" Of 1,500 businessmen
who replied to this question, 69 per cent said "yes." Forty-

seven per cent agreed "the American business executive tends to ignore the great ethical laws as they apply immediately to his work; he is preoccupied chiefly with gain."[12] Father Baumhart found unethical practices most flourishing in highly competitive industries. In all industries, certain companies are more unethical than others because senior executives set a bad example; subordinates who don't like playing monopoly with loaded dice drift away to another game. Father Baumhart, like Secretary Hodges, wishes more business leaders would take a serious interest in business ethics. At a National Association of Manufacturers committee meeting in May, 1963, he deplored the rationalizing done by two out of five of his businessman contacts, who had admitted they were resigned to a situation described as follows:

> "Competition today is stiffer than ever; as a result, many businessmen find themselves forced to resort to practices which are considered shady, but which appear necessary to survive."[13]

If the success ethic is indeed losing its appeal, the pressures for conformity within companies and industries that support such attitudes should soon begin to weaken. A few non-conformists are being heard from now. That well-known elder statesman of business, Clarence B. Randall, chides managements for failing to realize that "in a free society a man good enough to make a strong contribution is good enough to have his own scale of values, and that goals which he has established for the total achievement of

his own life are not necessarily parallel with those which
management has proclaimed for the company."[14]

The importance of this kind of independence is the
theme of a highly personal book by Kermit Eby, *Protests
of an Ex-Organization Man.* "I have worked in organizations and have compromised," Eby admits. "I continue to
do so daily and I teach my students that compromise is
often necessary in a choice between conflicting principles.
But I also teach them that there is a point at which man
must respect his sense of a higher morality and stand beyond compromise."[15]

This is precisely the message of a play which was a hit in
London and New York with both critics and, surprisingly,
the public. *A Man for All Seasons* portrays the martyrdom
of St. Thomas More as a moral lesson for the twentieth
century. The playwright, Robert Bolt, explains in a preface
to the bookstore edition that he is concerned about living in
a society in which the only certainty is the supreme value
of getting and spending. Men no longer possess a sense of
self. The result: "there are fewer and fewer things which,
as they say, we 'cannot bring ourselves' to do."

In contrast to Plastic Man, Bolt continues,

> Thomas More, as I wrote about him, became for me
> a man with an adamantine sense of his own self. He
> knew where he began and left off, what area of him-
> self he could yield to the encroachments of his ene-
> mies, and what to the encroachments of those he
> loved. It was a substantial area in both cases, for he
> had a proper sense of fear and was a busy lover. Since

he was a clever man and a great lawyer he was able to
retire from those areas in wonderfully good order, but
at length he was asked to retreat from that final area
where he located his self. And there this supple, humorous, unassuming and sophisticated person set like
metal, was overtaken by an absolutely primitive rigor,
and could no more be budged than a cliff.[16]

This is why Bolt, who describes himself as not even a
Christian in the usual sense, placed Thomas More rever-
ently in the Broadway spotlight four centuries after his
martyrdom.

Upon seeing *A Man for All Seasons* in Chicago, I was
reminded that I had described Thomas More as "The Organization Saint" in a magazine sketch several years before.
The "organization" within which Thomas More had to
operate was the Tudor monarchy. The problem he faced in
the sixteenth century was the same one you may have
struggled with yesterday afternoon at the office: how can a
man co-exist with authority that does not share his principles? The main difference was that in his day the boss
could cut off your head as well as your pay. In his book,
Utopia, More offered counsel on picking your way warily
through an arbitrary and unpredictable world:

You must not . . . abandon the ship of state and
desert it in a storm, because you cannot control the
winds . . . By indirect approach and covert suggestion
you must endeavor . . . to handle all well, and what
you cannot turn to good, you must make as little bad

as you can. For it is impossible that all should be well, unless all men are good, which I do not expect for a great many years to come.

More followed this advice from the mouth of one of his fictional characters as long as he could, in small matters as well as affairs of state. At one point, Henry VIII became so fond of More's charming and witty company that he insisted on having him around almost all the time. More's son-in-law, William Roper, recorded More's reaction:

> Because he was of a pleasant disposition, it pleased the king and queen. . . . at the time of their supper. . . . commonly to call for him to be merry with them. Whom when he perceived so much in his talk to delight, that he could not once in a month get leave to go him to his wife and children (whose company he most desired) . . . he, misliking this restraint of his liberty, began thereupon somewhat to dissemble his nature, and so by little and little from his former accustomed mirth to disuse himself, that he was of them from thenceforth at such seasons no more so ordinarily sent for.[17]

Given such an intimate opportunity to cultivate the boss, most men would capitalize on it in any century. More, shrewd enough not to antagonize Henry, was unwilling to sacrifice his family life to ambition. Fortunately, there are men today who similarly set limits to their ambition.

Sloan Wilson, whose novel *The Man in the Gray Flan-*

nel Suit, provided polemicists with an endlessly useful symbol while making gray flannel suits as extinct as sport jackets with belts in the back, now sees a shift in attitude away from the earlier uncritical acceptance of the success ethic which he dramatized. In a magazine article published in 1962, he credited the example of serious-minded young people who, less interested in wealth than their upward struggling parents had been, are studying to be physicians or teachers or scientists. They don't want to work for "money alone." And the now aging prototype suburbanite with a gray flannel taste in his mouth is having second thoughts. Wilson reported:

> Several of our families, for instance, dropped out of the country club, where the parties had been getting kind of wild, and saved their money for a trip abroad. A close friend of mine gave up a profitable job at an advertising agency to become the treasurer of a small college where he felt he could be more useful, and in several cases people moved from large, showy houses into smaller ones, just to get rid of some of the financial pressure. All of a sudden many of us began taking extension courses at a local college, and conversations at cocktail parties centered less on golf or the upkeep of lawns, more on recordings and books, including some which weren't even on the best-seller list.[18]

Academic friends of mine have suggested that from advertising to college administration is not necessarily the path of virtue, but Wilson isn't claiming suburbia is prepared to embrace poverty, chastity, and obedience. He merely senses the beginning of changes which already make Cadillacs seem a bit vulgar and offer hope for greater maturity in the future.

Katherine Anne Porter recalls that when she was a girl she wrote a letter to her sister "saying I wanted glory. I don't know quite what I meant by that now, but it was something different from fame or success or wealth."[19]

There is evidence today that many men are groping for something different from fame or success or wealth. The search, although difficult, may very well end in glory.

NOTES

1. *Science News Letter*, May 11, 1963.
2. *Chicago Daily News*, February 12, 1963.
3. *Chicago Daily News*, March 7, 1963.
4. *Advertising Age*, September 11, 1963.
5. Esther Milner, *The Failure of Success*. New York: Exposition, 1959.
6. John Cogley, "A New Breed of Cat," *Commonweal*, March 8, 1963.
7. Milner, *op. cit.*
8. Sargent Shriver, "I Have the Best Job in Washington," *New York Times Magazine*, June 9, 1963.
9. Clarence B. Randall, "U.S. Problem: Low Pay for Top Jobs," *New York Times Magazine*, September 15, 1963.
10. Englewood Cliffs, N. J.: Prentice-Hall, 1963.
11. *The New World*, August 2, 1963.
12. Rev. Raymond C. Baumhart, S.J., "Business Ethics," New York Clergy-Industry Relations Department, National Association of Manufacturers, 1963.

13. *Ibid.*

14. Clarence B. Randall, *The Folklore of Management.* New York: Mentor, 1962.

15. Boston: Beacon Press, 1961.

16. New York: Random House, 1962.

17. William Roper, *The Life of Sir Thomas More, Knight.* (Now available in Everyman's Library edition.)

18. Sloan Wilson, "Look What's Happened to the Man in the Gray Flannel Suit," *Suburbia Today,* October, 1962.

19. *Writers at Work: The Paris Review Interviews.* Second series. Introduced by Van Wyck Brooks. New York: Viking, 1963.

8

Woman's Work Is Never Fun

Failure is usually thought of as a masculine prerogative. This is an outmoded prejudice, which in this day of equal rights for women must be rejected. In fact, failure is probably another of the many activities in which women excel the performance of men.

If a woman pursues a career in the world without marrying, she has to pretend she doesn't care that others pity her for becoming an old maid. If she marries, she scarcely has time to hang the curtains before neo-feminists are berating her for not developing her potential as an individual through a career.

The first woman executive in the history of the Interplanetary Corporation reacted with mixed emotions to the announcement of her promotion. She was delighted, of course, with the increase in pay, a new title, new authority and the approval of past efforts that a promotion implies. But in telling her of the company's decision Hector Gladly was not especially tactful. "You know, Interplanetary never gave a big job like this to a woman before. Women are always getting married and having babies and such, just when we need them. But you're different, Miss Mudturtle. We know we can count on you to stick by us."

Mildred Mudturtle managed to retain her composure for the rest of the day at the office, but that night at home she called her married sister for comfort and wept into the telephone. A promotion that hinged partly on the company's assessment of her as unmarriageable wasn't quite her dream come true.

The episode ruined her sister's evening, too. Dorothy envied Mildred's freedom. While Mildred led an exciting, stimulating life in business, Dorothy was being put upon by three children and a husband who traveled frequently on business. While Mildred took glamorous vacations with her savings, Dorothy was stuck at home conversing mainly with five-year-olds. News of Mildred's promotion set Dorothy wondering again whether she could have made a name for herself if she had followed the interior decorating career she once planned.

"The American woman is criticized no matter what she does," says Dr. Helen Lopata, Roosevelt University sociologist. "She either is called overly protective of her children or a gadabout. She either is blamed for taking over too many of a man's jobs or for driving her husband to an early grave."[1]

Women long have had grounds for just complaint. It wasn't until 1920 that the nineteenth amendment gave American women the right to vote, which seemed to be the culmination of the feminist movement. In recent years there has been a revival of agitation for other rights as a new generation of spokesmen (rather, spokeswomen) complained about educational and cultural factors that combine to keep women subjugated, despite some progress in legal status and career opportunities.

Simone de Beauvoir's book *The Second Sex,* which appeared in English in 1953, seems to have inspired a wave of neo-feminism which keeps many educated women in a chronic state of discontent. Mme. de Beauvoir complains that failure is built into a woman's psyche.

> Even when (woman) chooses independence, she none the less makes a place in her life for man, for love. She is likely to fear that if she devotes herself completely to some undertaking, she will miss her womanly destiny. This feeling often remains unavowed, but it is there; it weakens well-defined purposes, it sets limits.[2]

On the other hand, a young woman can in only a few weeks, by maneuvering a successful doctor or executive into marriage, achieve far greater social status and financial well-being than she could obtain from a lifetime of striving on her own. If a young man can take a short cut to the top by marrying the boss's daughter, a woman can get there faster by marrying the boss himself (and becoming that young smart alec's mother-in-law). Neo-feminists lament this apparent advantage for women because the ease of the sexual route to status and comfort deprives them of independence and enterprise.

The tension in women's lives between the desire for marriage and the attraction of individual accomplishment can no longer be resolved in the traditional way. You can't tell a woman who during her youth has acquired a college degree or two, a driver's license, perhaps even a flying license, that her place is in the home, darning socks. Cardinal Suenens of Belgium, one of many who recognize that the revolutionary changes of our times include a new status for women, has written:

> The classical picture in which initiative lies with the man, and woman's part is submission, is no longer current. Penelope at her weaving, Marguerite at her spinning-wheel, Juliet on her balcony, Sister Anne shut up in her tower living on expectation . . . nowadays they all smack of folklore.
>
> There is nothing in this advancement as such that militates in Christian eyes against the subordination to her husband in the home demanded by St. Paul, but this subordination can no longer be validly carried over to the whole of life. . . . She no longer acts through man by her influence on him, but in her own right and under her own colors.[3]

To admit that woman's situation is changing does not solve her problems. Some of the solutions being proposed are as unrealistic as those quaint old woodcuts of perpetual motion machines. And the neo-feminists tend to speak with an unappealing stridency. Simone de Beauvoir would abolish marriage. Betty Friedan, whose book, *The Feminine Mystique*, sold 65,000 copies in hardcover, then appeared as a paperback in every drugstore, believes marriage should be fitted into a woman's career like a hobby. She cites approvingly a study of Vassar seniors preparing for various professions who nearly all plan to marry, "but marriage is for them an activity in which they will voluntarily choose to participate rather than something that is necessary for any sense of personal identity."[4] Mrs. Friedan doesn't mind if women get married, but she doesn't think they should get involved in marriage.

Indeed, she herself confesses receiving a fright as a college girl upon winning a fellowship. "We walked in the Berkeley hills and a boy said: 'Nothing can come of this, between us. I'll never win a fellowship like yours.' Did I think I would be choosing, irrevocably, the cold loneliness of that afternoon if I went on? I gave up the fellowship, in relief." But her mature opinion is that a woman, even if married, "should compete impersonally in society, as men do" rather than "compete for dominance in her own home."[5]

American women, whatever their degree of response to neo-feminism, are not accepting Mme. de Beauvoir's rejection of marriage. In 1960, 93 per cent of American women in their thirties had been married at least once. Comparable percentages for other countries indicated a lower romance quotient: 82 per cent in Britain, 72 in France and 55 in Ireland.[6] They're marrying young, too, often without finishing the educations that would prepare them for careers, a fact which would have greatly distressed Susan B. Anthony and the other suffragettes who fought so hard for women's rights.

Some educators believe higher education is wasted on

women. At a time when the educational system strains to
meet the demands placed upon it, they say women tend to
coast through college with no real commitment to any field
of learning, to marry as soon as possible and retire to housewifery, making no use of the education society helped provide them. This infuriates the neo-feminists, who insist that
women have been brainwashed in recent years to accept
housewifery as their sole destiny, in contrast to the valiant
rebels of an earlier generation.

Women who attempt careers in addition to marriage, as
Betty Friedan would have it in her revision for conventional American tastes of the Beauvoir Plan, face all the
same frustrations as men, plus special obstacles designed
just for them. There is plain prejudice, reflected in lower
pay and fewer promotions. I know of one company where
male employees are encouraged to retire early but women
must work to the last scheduled hour. Even those companies determined to treat women fairly have second
thoughts about placing married women in positions of responsibility. Male executives quit, causing the company
inconvenience, but for fewer reasons. Women also have
babies or move to another city suddenly because their husbands were transferred.

The same women most likely to attempt to combine
marriage and career are most likely to belong to the most
mobile part of the population. In the suburb where I live,
30 per cent of the homes change hands every year, and a
substantial number of the sellers move out of the state. It
has been suggested that if a woman has an especially good
job, the husband should consider turning down his own

promotion, transfer, or new job offer in the interests of the neo-feminist ideal of domestic equality.

Unfortunately, a man ordinarily does not encounter more than a few opportunities to rise in the organizational society. To pass up a good offer for the sake of his wife's career is risky. He will be expected to support the family year in and year out, long after the arrival of a child, or perhaps twins, has undermined the employability of his lady vice president.

One possible solution to this difficulty is for husbands and wives to be employed as teams. Husband-wife teams have achieved high distinction already in a number of fields, including scientific research (the Curies), drama (the Lunts), literature (the Brownings), journalism (the Goulds), and politics (the Roosevelts). When a company wanted a new manager for the Omaha branch office, it could appoint a husband-wife combination. Then both would be willing to make the move. And regardless of whether one or the other has a flare-up of his ulcers or an acute case of pregnancy the office will be almost certain of having a manager on duty.

Of course, this will present certain problems in education. Courting will have to be limited to boys and girls studying the same major. It would never do to have an incipient physicist dating a drama major, and mixed marriages between the school of business and the liberal arts college must be strictly prohibited.

Neo-feminists sneer at men who would object to working under the supervision of a qualified woman, just because of her sex. Such men are weak, they say. This seems unfair to me. Organizational competition is a sublimated form of aggression, in which the participants hurl barbed memos instead of bashing each other with clubs. The woman who participates freely in this melee is an especially unattractive figure to men, who have been bred in the bone to expect a soothing touch from a woman's hand, not a rabbit punch. It may be necessary, in order to be fair, to give women the same opportunities for advancement in the chain of command as men, but men can't be expected to like it. The average man, already virtually overwhelmed by the intensity of competition from only half the population, will then find every hand against him—that of his secretary most of all.

Is success in competition of this type necessary for self-fulfillment? In the Christian tradition the chief struggle is against the self. Simone de Beauvoir complains that present circumstances require women to forget the self. She seems annoyed that Mary described herself willingly as the "handmaid" of the Lord. She writes tartly, "The Catholic religion among others exerts a most confused influence upon the young girl."[7]

The idea that a woman, like a man, profits by handing over the self to God gets short shrift from Mrs. Friedan, who dismisses it as "an age-old panacea."[8] Morton M. Hunt, whose contribution to the neo-feminist bookshelf, *Her Infinite Variety: The American Woman As Lover, Mate & Rival*, was a Book-of-the-Month Club selection, criticizes a speech by Pope Pius XII for being reminiscent of *Animal Farm*. The late pontiff had merely restated the traditional Christian teaching that men and women are equal, but that the husband is the head of the wife. All the neo-feminists consider the home a cell, not in a cloister of peace, but in a prison.

Simone de Beauvoir reports wives thinking in "anguish: 'Only this, forever! Forever this husband, this dwelling.' "[9] Mrs. Friedan poses the same question in almost the same words: "You are born, you grow, you are impregnated, you have a child, it grows . . . but is this all there is to life for a woman today?"[10]

A Harvard University research team has found that the riskiest time for mental disorder among mothers is during the three months following childbirth.[11] The type of women most often seen in clinics with a "neurotic depressive reaction" to domesticity has been described by Dr. Donald Paull, chief psychologist of Forest Hospital, as follows: "About 35 years old, with two pre-kindergarten children . . . perhaps have had two or three years of college."[12] Dr. Paull explains that such women often are distressed to discover that their real circumstances in life do not match the self-conception they formed for themselves as girls.

As shown in earlier chapters, the prevalent woman's illusion that her husband is enjoying a fascinating and satisfying career while she drudges at home cannot be related to reality. But unfair differences in their lives do exist. If a man somehow finds a foxhole in life where the frustrations are tolerable, he may be permitted to crawl in out of the line of fire and relax with his hard-won peace. If a wife achieves a degree of accommodation, she'll be told by a thousand voices that she can't really be happy, she's only kidding herself. Paradoxically, despite sincere concern for the problems of women, the neo-feminists tend to make the problems worse. They are often professional malcontents to whom success in a career is the only success.

Simone de Beauvoir and Morton M. Hunt both compare women to Negroes as an oppressed class. Telling women to be happy in their traditional roles as wives and mothers, they say, is like telling Negroes they should have been happy with the security of slavery.

One woman who considers herself fulfilling God's plan for her through her life in the home wearies of the complaints of frustrated housewives. "I realize that there are women who have real problems to contend with, and I sympathize with them, but I have nothing but scorn for those who have good husbands, nice homes, few financial worries, and still are unhappy. Phooey to all of them!" Instead of agreeing with this pearl of common sense, Hunt comments that women like this take motherhood too seriously and are prone to "overattachment, overprotection and overmothering."[13]

Another woman who finds her life happy and fulfilling says, "Children are a source of endless delight and consternation. But delight far outshines consternation! Once we've known the joy of motherhood, even the annoyances and worries that go with child raising can't discourage us from wanting more babies. . . . In a mother's heart there is always room for one more." Hunt finds this "saccharine" and adds, "If a statement like that is uttered or read aloud to any group of intelligent and sophisticated modern women, many of them will feel faintly embarrassed."[14]

Betty Friedan doesn't believe in happy housewives either. "Like Diogenes with his lamp, I went as a reporter from suburb to suburb, searching for a woman of ability and education who was fulfilled as a housewife." She didn't find any, which was not surprising, since she recognizes only two classes of housewives: frustrated intellectuals and "moms"—psychological monsters whose children would be better off left with the maid.

The housewife looking for contentment at home, she adds, is a "sex-seeker." She digs up evidence that the most traditionally feminine women are the most trouble to psychiatrists. She scorns the college marriage courses, parent education programs, prenatal and child-study groups of recent years for contributing to the "feminine mystique." She dismisses these aids to family life as Freudian functionalism, "sounding a single, overprotective, life-restricting, future-denying note for women."[15]

A famous study several years ago turned up 50 "normal" males in Minneapolis schools, young men completely free of any signs of personality disorder. Later on, Dr. Jules S. Golden and Reuben J. Silver of Albany (N.Y.) Medical College and Dr. Nathan Mandel of the Minnesota state department of correction studied the wives of the first thirty-eight to marry. They are some of the happy housewives Betty Friedan couldn't find. The thirty-eight young wives turned out, if anything, even better adjusted socially and economically than their husbands. The investigators reported:

Our data indicate that they experience what we consider some of life's deepest and most meaningful pleasures in their stable relationships with each other as well as in raising their children. Such a population would promote stability and a firm backbone for our country.[16]

The investigators added that these normal couples are rather unimaginative and lead routine, dull lives. In other words, except for their emotional stability, they are like all the other unimaginative Americans who lead dull, routine lives. I thought the charge of dullness was a gratuitous insult, considering that electrifying, imaginative personalities must be at least as scarce as emotionally stable types.

Since these women are not frustrated and obviously cannot be accused of "momism," would this research persuade the neo-feminists that perhaps housewifery is not so bad? Of course not. Aha, comes the answer, if you really are a happy housewife, it's because you're too stupid to know better. Rena Corman (who incidentally has collaborated with Hunt on a book about psychoanalysis) develops this idea in an article about the thirty-eight normal wives.

These Golden few may be normal only because they have neither education, nor stimulation, nor stress, nor imagination. In fact, perhaps they are not only few but on their way to becoming extinct.

Ah, well, let them die out—along with the illiterate peasant women of an earlier age, who enjoyed the simple sunshine, their babies' sucking at their breasts, the chattering of other women as together they beat their clothes against the rocks along the shore, and little else.[17]

Through the ages, children have been a source of joy for women when few other satisfactions were available to them. In the neo-feminist scheme, children are only slightly more welcome than a gall-bladder attack. In a chapter on "The Independent Woman," Mme. de Beauvoir expresses sympathy for the career woman who, having failed to take advantage of contraceptive techniques, "finds herself responsible for an unwanted child that can ruin her professional life."[18]

Mrs. Friedan, who admits having felt "half-guilty" about leaving her three children while she went off to work outside the home, joyfully cites surveys showing that children of working mothers are no worse off psychologically than children of full-time mothers. She argues that having a full-time mother is bad for children, because of "a kind of infantilism that makes the children of the housewife-mothers incapable of the effort, the endurance of pain and frustration, the discipline needed to compete on the baseball field, or get into college."[19]

She thinks women should insist on more day nurseries with professional staffs and other changes in the rules to make it easier for women to follow careers. She seriously proposes a sort of GI Bill that would provide "qualified women" with books, tuition and babysitters while they pursued or resumed their educations.

There is a real tension between marriage and a career

interest for women with special talents. Marriage means dropping out of their field just when they've made a good beginning, growing rusty at home while others forge ahead, then trying to come back to it twenty years later with virtually amateur standing. But why do so many commentators assume that marriage necessarily estranges a woman from the life of the intellect? Simone de Beauvoir sets the style with her description of marriage as "a thousand evenings of vague small talk, blank silences, yawning over the newspaper, retiring at bedtime. . . . Whether the husband succeeds in making the wife an echo of himself or each one is entrenched within a private universe, after some months or years they have nothing left to say to one another."[20] Ignace Lepp, a French priest and psychiatrist, laments how often he has seen brilliant girl students atrophy into banality after a few years of marriage. Marriage is dull, he says, because "the feeling develops gradually that one's husband or wife is less susceptible of being moved by the great and beautiful things of life than a friend whom one sees from time to time when he has a positive desire to do so."[21]

In this age of easily available books and periodicals there is no reason why a woman can't maintain her intellectual interests despite marriage and children. She's busy? Everybody's busy. If her intellectual interests were superficial to begin with, she'll always be too occupied with trivia to read a difficult book. The statement "I never have time to read" is incomprehensible to chronic readers, who long ago learned to read at lunch, while walking along the sidewalk (always look up for crossings), while waiting for the doctor.

As for life in the home, the woman has more influence over its character than the man. Unless she married a clod, which is a different problem, she can find ways to make conversations more stimulating if she wants to.

A woman writer of my acquaintance once said in a speech:

"Instead of complaining that she doesn't have the opportunity to fulfill herself, a woman might better organize herself. Whatever she truly wants to do, she will do."

I happen to know that this woman manages to keep up her own intellectual interests while coping with eight children, a husband who saves things, a sly dog, a fluctuating population of guinea pigs, and a ten-room house. After being married to her for fourteen years, I find her conversation more stimulating, not less, in proportion to the widening scope of her reading and the greater maturity of her thought. This probably is truer to life for a great many couples than the conventional portrait of husband and wife who, after many years of marriage, have nothing to say to each other.

Many women make their own troubles by allowing housework to expand to fill all their available time. Jean Libman Block, a novelist, wife and mother who wrote a magazine article specifically to refute Betty Friedan, said:

> Housework needn't be a trap. I suspect the woman who complains most about the boredom of dishwashing and bedmaking is basically a boring person. Otherwise, she'd get the chores done quickly (why all those appliances?) and turn to something that interests her.[22]

One reason housewives are dispirited is that they are victims of the same utilitarian outlook as men. They feel apologetic about anything they do that doesn't earn money. Making ceramics in a basement kiln is only amateur dabbling, but selling someone else's ceramics part-time in the neighborhood gift shop is a worth-while job, and writing ads full-time for someone else's ceramics for the department store downtown is a career. Scarcely anyone considers this a reversal of values.

The Survey Research Center of the University of Michigan found that three-fourths of working women said they would keep at it even if they inherited a comfortable independent income.[23] Exactly the attitude of men.

I can't help thinking of Benjamin Franklin, whose life was in many ways similar to that of modern woman. While young he worked seven days a week. Then at the age of forty-two, about the time a woman's family responsibilities usually decrease, he considered himself financially secure. So he retired from business to devote himself to true leisure: science, invention, and politics. It was significant that Franklin refused to profit financially from his many useful inventions. In his day, the classical understanding of leisure had not yet perished.

Educators are working out ways to help women follow Franklin's example. Alex Rosen, dean of the New York University School of Social Work, says:

> With early marriage, completion of the family when the mother is still in her thirties, and with increased longevity, it is possible for women in this

technological age to have two full careers, as a mother
and as a professional.[24]

In the long run a solution along this line might please
even the neo-feminists, who will never be able to find
enough nursery schools and babysitters to permit large
numbers of women to juggle motherhood and careers simultaneously. And it doesn't seem likely that there will be a
stampede to dedicated spinsterhood, much as this might do
to alleviate both the shortage of skilled workers and the
population problem.

But there is one last word to say about women. They are
no more likely than men to find happiness in the pursuit of
selfish interests. In the past, the circumstances of the typical
woman's life demanded generosity from her to a degree
seldom required of a man. It has always been the wife who
left old associations to go where her husband goeth and
cook dinner the way he likes it. When the baby cried at
three o'clock in the morning, it has always been the mother
who got up and comforted it. Unless she rebelled entirely,
she had to be generous. Her husband, meanwhile, could eat
and sleep like a hog if he wanted to without attracting
criticism from the neighbors, or even his mother-in-law, as
long as he earned a comfortable living.

To say that in this situation the woman has the advantage can be misunderstood. It sounds too much like the
pietistic old ladies who tell the neighborhood children they
should be glad they skinned their knees because now they
have something to offer up. Still, the Christian paradox
cannot be ignored. It *is* better to give than to receive.

The patriarchal family is disappearing, and in the new family pattern that is emerging women inevitably will enjoy new freedoms. They will be increasingly able to plan their lives rationally to take advantage of whatever artistic and intellectual potentialities they possess. But, if the neo-feminists persuade them they should make their husbands do the cooking for the sake of careers, they'll be disillusioned in time.

Freya Stark, a woman whose travel books are literature, is conspicuously absent from the ranks of the neo-feminists. From her glimpses of many cultures, some far less advanced than our own, she concludes: "Civilization, which requires feminine time and attention, seems to suffer and decline where women work very hard."[25]

If the generality of women become as hardened as the generality of men, they will have failed indeed.

NOTES

1. *Chicago Daily News*, January 17, 1964.
2. *The Second Sex*. Translated and edited by H. M. Parshley. New York: Knopf, 1953.
3. *The Nun in the World*. Revised edition. Westminster, Md.: Newman, 1963.
4. *The Feminine Mystique*. New York: Norton, 1963.
5. *Ibid.*
6. Marion K. Sanders, "Case of the Vanishing Spinster." *New York Times Magazine*, September 22, 1963.
7. *Op. cit.*
8. *Op. cit.*
9. *Op. cit.*

10. *Op. cit.*

11. *Science News Letter*, June 22, 1963.

12. *Arlington Heights (Ill.) Herald*, October 24, 1963.

13. *Her Infinite Variety: the American Woman as Lover, Mate & Rival.* New York: Harper & Row, 1962.

14. *Ibid.*

15. *Op. cit.*

16. Rena Corman, "Close-up of the 'Normal' Wife." *New York Times Magazine*, September 8, 1963.

17. *Ibid.*

18. *Op. cit.*

19. *Op. cit.*

20. *Op. cit.*

21. *The Psychology of Loving.* Translated by Bernard B. Gilligan. Baltimore: Helicon, 1963.

22. "Who Says U.S. Women Are 'Trapped'?" *This Week*, October 6, 1963.

23. Daniel Bell, "The Great Back-to-Work Movement." *Fortune*, July, 1956.

24. *New York Times*, March 10, 1964.

25. *The Journey's Echo: Selections from Freya Stark.* Foreword by Lawrence Durrell. New York: Harcourt, Brace & World, 1964.

9

Handbook for Husbands

Chances are, you bungled your wedding night like everything else. Most men do, according to surveys and psychological case histories. It is difficult for a decent man to be anything but a bungler, since the alternative seems to be coming to the occasion with experience.

Perhaps this is a clue to some of the tensions of our times. It used to be easier for a man to choose his failures. He could leave Xantippe triumphant at the hearth while he tried to make a name for himself in the agora. Or, if he had been imprudent enough to politic against George Washington, he could withdraw from public affairs and run a tight ship at home. Nowadays, the odds are you won't cut much of a figure either place.

A considerable body of opinion holds that marriage has tended toward failure ever since Western man began trying to combine marriage with love. Father Ignace Lepp says:

Priests, psychologists, doctors and other recognized counsellors know how rarely it is possible today to say of marriages, a few years after they have been contracted, that they have been completely successful and that they have contributed to the further normal development of each of the two partners.[1]

Victor Neumark, former chairman of the Chicago Bar Association committee on matrimonial law, estimates that only one marriage in twenty-one is happy.

Virtually all marriages are contracted between two persons who are too self-centered and immature to undertake such a close relationship. It might be hoped that the novelty of their romance will tide them over until they have time to grow up a little. Unfortunately, the pressures of the times devalue the dignity of age and prolong adolescence and adolescent attitudes, and not everyone continues to grow toward maturity after the age of marriage.

Current emphasis on sexual adjustment is almost hysterical. Such writers as Simone de Beauvoir go on at length about how sexual initiation can be a traumatic experience for the wife if handled clumsily. Discussion centers on whether the wife has satisfactory orgasms, with the implication that her husband is a failure if she doesn't. Readers of fiction, in which sex is almost universally presented as titillating, must assume there is something wrong with their own marriages.

The facts seem to be that many wives never have orgasms; of those wives who do have orgasms, few reach this climax on every occasion. The normal thing is for a couple's sexual adjustment to improve gradually over a period of time as they grow closer in love and understanding. Any initial problems often work themselves out. This relationship is the source of many a private joke: sometimes it expresses tenderness and unity beyond description, other times a neighbor contrives to smash his car into the side of his garage at the worst possible moment or old friends drop in unexpectedly. A husband who retains his sense of humor can survive, but if he takes this subject as seriously as some writers he may be persuaded that he is a failure at the one thing only a man can do.

A new husband is concerned also about establishing his position as leader in his family. He can no longer automatically assume the authoritarian role of long ago. Although surveys show that the middle-class husband still holds a slight edge, the contemporary family pattern gives both partners nearly equal voice. His wife has been educated to make up her own mind on every conceivable question. If he complains that he expected a more submissive partner, she may tell him, using the latest psychological jargon, that he's only seeking a mother figure and for Pete's sake grow up. If he thought he was going to run his household like a platoon of Marines, he's a failure before he begins.

Marriage is not an arena for slugging out the issue of dominance. It is rather a school, where each partner instructs the other on growth in generosity. In former times, men often married much younger women and set themselves up to instruct them in all areas of life. I was delighted to read about a fourteenth-century husband, the Ménagier

de Paris, who wrote a whole book of instructions for his
wife covering religious and moral duties, household management, cookery, and a compilation of games and amusements. It included such sage counsels as these:

> Have a care that you be honestly clad, without new
> devices and without too much or too little frippery . . .
> Remember the rustic proverb, which saith that there
> be three things which drive the goodman from home,
> to wit, a dripping roof, a smoking chimney and a
> scolding woman . . . In summer take heed that there
> be no fleas in your chamber nor in your bed, which
> you may do in six ways, as I have heard tell . . . If you
> have another husband after me, know that you should
> think much of his comfort . . . cherish the person of
> your husband carefully and, I pray you, keep him in
> clean linen.[2]

Any husbands who would like to so instruct their wives
nowadays are free to try, but the attempt will probably
cost them more than it's worth. A more practical approach
to a twentieth-century version of the Ménagier de Paris'
book would be a manual on the proper care of wives that a
man keeps in a secret place and refers to from time to time
for his own benefit.

To be kept in a secret place it would have to be a very
small book. That's why I have kept the following outline
brief. If you find these suggestions helpful, you might have
them engraved on the underside of your cuff links.

Chapter 1. Wife-Reassurance. Woman needs reassurance

because circumstances of her life make her feel insecure in many situations. Praise and encouragement at the right times enable any human being to accomplish more than he or she thought possible. Husband should not criticize cooking or housekeeping. Big mouths who make fun of their wives in public should shut up or stay home. (They only bore the other guests anyway.) The lump who never notices anything his wife does, consequently can't praise it, should take cold showers and wake up.

Chapter 2. Communication. Classic subject for marriage counselors who find many couples don't get along because they never communicate with each other. In well-balanced marriages, partners may guard tongues against words that sting, but they talk things out. Then the matter is settled instead of lying on the air for days like the odor of a dead cigar. One counselor used to advise extreme cases to have two telephones installed in the house. Then, when communication faltered, one spouse could dial the other. Americans will talk at length about anything on the telephone.

Chapter 3. Wife-Education. If she never has a chance to think about anything but housework, children, and the neighbors, she won't talk about anything but housework, children, and neighbors. If your only interests are business, baseball and cars, social life will work out smoothly. When you're together in company she can talk to the women and you can talk to the men. But if you have more extensive interests, you won't find this satisfactory. It will profit you to make sure she has access to books and magazines. And take her out occasionally to a stimulating show or lecture. Your efforts in this area will be repaid in good conversation at home. You might even learn something yourself.

It takes time, of course, to pursue your wife's education. This brings up the fourth chapter of the "Handbook for Husbands," which concerns the resultant of the centrifugal force that sends a man out into the world and the centripetal force that brings him home again. A cunning husband can always find excuses not to go home. The boss wants him to work late because of a meeting first thing next morning. The client likes to stand around and drink while he talks business and works up nerve to sign the contract. "After all, honey, it's only for you and the children; we'll have more time for each other some day."

That day, of course, never comes. If it did, there'd be nothing to talk about, just as the neo-feminists predicted in the last chapter.

The opposite of the go-getter is the secret loafer. (I can see that the "Handbook" won't fit under your cuff links after all.) In our times there are too many pressures that prevent a man from loafing around the house and failing to support his family for him to reveal his true nature. But he can avoid involvement with work as much as possible. He can use his natural interest in his home life as an excuse for not facing up to his responsibilities in economic and political life.

Some observers thought a weakness like this underlay the "togetherness" movement of recent years. "Togetherness," as it was usually interpreted apart from its advertising usage, did not mean the delight in companionship that is one of the greatest blessings of marriage. On the contrary, it was a perversion in which the husband became a sort of assistant woman. The movement collapsed when it turned out there wasn't any real need for assistant women.

The chapter about work versus togetherness should deal also with love. For some inexplicable reason, very little is written or said about love in marriage from the man's point of view, except to lecture husbands about not pressing too hard for their rights. Is it assumed that the wife does all the loving and the husband is interested only in board and bed? This is not the fact. Men, like all human creatures, feel the need for love and can be pitiful in their eagerness for it. They also need to be able to give love.

"Individuals who really know how to love are actually very rare," says Father Lepp. "They are much rarer even than those who really know how to think."[3] A great lover is not a Don Juan. Psychology has shown this type to be a psychotic weakling. Nor is a great lover someone who experiences a great emotion.

Love is an act of the will which, in marriage, shows its greatest strength. Father Lepp can bring himself to write about "marriage, the enemy of love." The difficulty is partly semantic. "Love" is one of those words everyone knows the meaning of until you attempt to define it to the satisfaction of someone else. Then no one knows its meaning. If love means a progressive enlightenment of the heart (in Franz Weyergans' beautiful phrase: "If you have not known the temptation to see in one beloved face the whole glory of God, you have not known love"[4]), then it only begins to gather force when the shallow passions of the honeymoon begin to ebb.

So, a husband must will to love from the beginning. Father Lepp observes: "He must know how to perform his role with an infinite amount of delicacy. In the first place, for example, it is not enough for a woman to know that she is loved. It is important that she *feel* it intensely."[5]

In the intense interaction of daily life together, the husband and wife, in a sense, create each other. By willing to love, the husband through the years creates a wife who is more lovable. She responds to his steadfast, will-directed love like a plant in the sunshine, sprouting new dimensions to her personality on the side where the sun shines brightest. Denied this atmosphere of beneficent warmth, she may wither into a bundle of thorns unless some unusual inner strength of her own protects her. The husband who harvests thorns can blame his gardening methods.

At a cocktail party, I directed a pleasantry at a friendly-looking man. In seconds, he was telling me all about his troubles with his wife. They had several small children who apparently were kept outdoors all summer like cattle. Every winter, when the weather required that they be admitted to the house, the wife felt the strain so intensely she had to receive psychiatric care. "Her trouble is she thinks the world owes her a living," the man said.

I immediately felt sorry for a man joined to a wife incapable of meeting the ordinary obligations that millions of other women make no particular fuss about. Then I reflected a moment on the mutuality of marriage. There is a streak of weakness and disloyalty in a man who would so criticize his wife before a stranger after only one drink, which raises the suspicion that he was failing his wife in some significant way that contributed to her instability.

Wise confessors have expressed speculative doubts that a husband or a wife can achieve salvation independently of one another. Once married, all their serious ventures are joint efforts. One hears frequently of the innocent, martyred wife whose husband drinks or cheats. Or of the long-suffering husband whose slatternly wife never learns to cook or keep house properly. If the whole truth were known, the apparent victim in a great many such cases is far from blameless. The same principle applies to the most profound depths of the two personalities joined in marriage.

Her spiritual life is yours, too.

Simone de Beauvoir in *The Second Sex* refers to woman as "the Other" at least thirty times, meaning that woman is set apart by male prejudice in a separate category of existence—a sort of alien who cannot expect the same rights as a citizen. But in marriage the wife is not the Other; she becomes the Self.

This is analogous to what happens at Mass when by partaking of the body and blood of Christ the members of the congregation reaffirm that they are one with Christ and therefore one with each other. For the Christian there is no Other. Marriage also is a sacrament, in which more happens than meets the eye. Whether the husband likes it or not his wife becomes attached to his Self symbiotically. She becomes his spiritual responsibility, and if he fails her he fails himself.

Paradoxically, there is little direct action a husband can take. He can't examine her conscience or deliver homilies at breakfast. If she has faults, his most promising maneuver is to redouble his efforts to combat his own faults. The strange symbiotic nature of marriage means that what he does about his own Self has an immediate and proportional effect on her Self, which is all part of the same Self anyhow.

Not everyone discovers this mechanism in marriage. I suppose there must be exceptions to its operation. However, most of the people who would claim it doesn't work are people who never have tried it to see.

I probably have seen more successful marriages than most observers. For a dozen years my wife and I have lent occasional aid and comfort to the Cana Conference of Chicago, an adult education organization built around couples whose intense commitment to marriage finds an outlet in working to bring a deeper understanding of marriage to other couples. In any given year a couple of hundred volunteer couples are engaged in conducting the program, either as speakers or organizers. According to the expert consensus, these couples form an extraordinary group: their marriages are happy. No doubt, in the privacy of their homes Cana's public image of sweet reasonableness and lighthearted cheer sometimes gets clawed up in family spats. All marriages fail a little because two persons can never identify with each other completely. Even when they will to love with a large measure of generosity, they'll have stingy days. However, simple observation confirms that most of the time these couples practice what they preach, and it works.

They hold that marriage is important because every wife is the means of her husband's salvation, and vice versa. Faults in the spouse are to be expected, providing in fact the cross through which the partner atones for his sins and prepares to enter the heaven of which the love of husband and wife, reflecting the love of God, is a preview. There's nothing original about this idea, but when it sets the tone of a household a rare spirit of amity is generated. They love their neighbors, beginning with the nearest neighbor first: the spouse.

Conditions exist today for a deeper theological and psychological insight into marriage, inviting personal involvement in marriage by both partners to a degree seldom dreamed of when marriage was thought of primarily as a means of laying farms end to end. The world has glimpsed this happy land from a distance, but doesn't know quite how to get there. An imperfect apprehension of truth underlies the American penchant for marrying again and again after divorce.

Not everyone sees the vision, of course. Men and women often go through the formalities of weddings without becoming truly married. They remain separate individuals who happen to reside at the same address.

Newspapers are full of the names of prominent men who have succeeded well in their public lives—in business, politics, sports, the arts—but who are known to have failed in marriage. Forgetting that we instinctively know better, we feel such a failure is not important because the man in the news photo has become rich and famous in spite of it. Besides, a man is presumed to be less committed than a woman and more likely to build a life for himself apart from marriage.

This is possible only when no real marriage has been

attempted. In reality, failure in marriage is one of the most profound kinds of failure, either because the Self has been found wanting or because, on the brink of a great adventure, the Self proved timid.

NOTES

1. *The Psychology of Loving*. Translated by Bernard B. Gilligan. Baltimore: Helicon, 1963.
2. Eileen Power, *Medieval People*. New York: Doubleday-Anchor, 1954.
3. *Op. cit.*
4. *The Long Adventure*. Translated by Joseph Cunneen. Chicago: Regnery, 1960.
5. *Op. cit.*

10

The Knot in the Filial Tie

Having been passed over for promotion again, Treadwell sits brooding at his desk. He begins to imagine what his neighbors could be saying about him twenty or thirty years in the future:

"Old Treadwell never amounted to much himself, but he slaved to educate his boys. Now they're all doctors, lawyers, executives, generals, college presidents, Senators and such, and he's on easy street."

Treadwell feels a little better. He is succumbing to the Patriarch Complex with which fathers often comfort themselves at such times. His children, the Patriarch imagines, will accomplish everything he never managed to do himself, and their glory and profit will become his. The Patriarch tells himself that although he may have failed at everything else he won't fail as a parent.

Unfortunately, the Patriarch Complex is a delusion. It assumes a degree of gratitude that children seldom show their parents. Whatever capacity for generosity and sacrifice the children develop will be projected forward to their own children. If in later years Treadwell finds himself in desperate straits, his boys no doubt will rally round, especially if they think he still has a little insurance. The Senator might get him a job with the government. But as long as Treadwell can get by on his own, they'll be glad to let him.

Besides, regardless of the input of time, patience, tuition, and vitamins, with children there's no way of predicting the results. If you encourage a child to study medicine, he may become a skilled and dedicated physician. Or, as many overly ambitious parents have discovered, he may reject the idea so utterly that he won't even watch the cold-pill commercials on television.

It's just as easy to fail as a parent as in any other endeavor. There is much discussion in certain publications about whether parents should spank or not spank, give allowances or make children earn their spending money, insist on enrichment like music lessons and summer school or let children follow their own interests freely. The truth is, parents don't have as much control over the situation as they think.

The famous Gesell Institute pioneered research on the various stages of development children normally inflict upon their parents. In brief, the Gesell findings indicate that much of the time a child is sprouting wildly like an unmowed lawn during the spring rains, regardless of what his parents try to do about it. By the age of fifteen months, according to Gesell Institute researchers, the child already shows an insubordinate streak. It's a "dart and dash and fling age" when "a mere verbal 'No, No' has little effect."

At eighteen months, he won't come when called and seldom obeys any other command either. " 'No' is his chief word. . . . His interpersonal relations are almost completely dominated by ideas of taking."

Gesell findings on normal behavior patterns for other ages are equally unsettling:

Two and a half—"Rigid and inflexible . . . domineering and demanding. He must give the orders . . . an age of violent emotions."

Three and a half—"May blink his eyes, bite his nails, pick his nose, exhibit facial and other tics, masturbate, suck his thumb excessively . . . tremendous difficulties in relations with other people."

Four—"Language . . . guaranteed to shock . . . loves to defy parental commands . . . He swaggers, swears, boasts, defies."

Occasionally, there are brief moments of peace for parents. The Gesell Institute authorities say Five is an enjoyable age all round, warning ominously "while it lasts." Then back to normal. Six is "extremely difficult to deal with . . . extremely negative in his response to others. . . . He has to be right. He has to be praised. He has to win."

Seven—"More likely to complain than to rejoice . . . morose, mopey and moody. . . . Lips may curl downward in a permanent pout."

Eight—"Tendency to dramatize everything . . . tears and self-disparagement. 'I always do it wrong.' "

Nine—"More interested in friends than family . . . an age of considerable rebellion against authority."

If all this isn't enough to discourage parents from preening themselves over their children, the Gesell experts add

that after Ten children never again give parents "quite the
same whole-hearted and unreserved acceptance."[1] And this
is the fate of those who can be considered good parents.
For them there is hope of somehow producing, after
twenty years of good stages and bad, another generation of
young adults not noticeably worse than the last batch. For
less capable parents, the forces working against their
chances of success may prove overwhelming.

Fathers especially can be easily confused about what
they should be doing. The role of the father in the family
has been changing. The Victorian father considered his
children a species of wild animal upon which it was his
duty to impose civilization, by force if necessary. In the
1920s and 1930s there was less coercion, but father held the
child-care book open to the right page in one hand and his
watch in the other to make sure the children did the right
thing at the right time and never as much as fifteen minutes
"off schedule."

The reaction to all this was the permissive father of the
1940s and 1950s, who had to be seen to be believed. I saw
one once in typical inaction. He had brought his three-year-
old son to the playground. Presently, the child fell off a
swing. In some cultures, he would have borne it stoically as
part of his training to be a warrior. In others, he would
have wept while his father and any other passing grown-
ups fussed over him and distracted him with a crown of
flowers. This little boy's response was different: he picked
himself up, stomped over to his father and kicked him in
the shin.

I waited curiously to see whether this would strike the

father funny or spark a lightning bolt of paternal discipline. Neither. As soon as his pain apparently had receded, the father said weakly, "Now, Geoffrey, that was naughty. You mustn't do naughty things like that."

Fortunately, permissiveness and another fad, togetherness, have now run their course. Uncontrolled packs of little children running yelling through the house and kicking you in the shins were more than adult nerves could stand. The demands placed on fathers at present seem to be more sensible.

The typical middle-class father has more time, energy, money, education, and enthusiasm for his role than his father did. Dr. John J. Kane of the University of Notre Dame says: "The young American father of today is closer to his family and closer to reality. His warmth, affection and attention to his wife and children make the patriarch unnecessary and objectionable, and, if he had not already become so, obsolete." But, Dr. Kane cautions, "It is not all sweetness and light either, for despite improvements, there are liabilities, and the full impact of these changes is not yet clear."[2]

Dr. Margaret Mead, the distinguished anthropologist, doesn't think the existing American family is coping at all well with the entirely new problems of the space age. She has called for society to design "a new type of family life." One of her concerns is that the moral training of children has been taken over by mass media.[3]

It is true parents seem to feel less and less competent to set standards for their children's behavior. This is seen in the rapid spread of formal codes of behavior for teens.

Edward Linzer, education director of the National Association for Mental Health, says:

"A number of parents are weak when it comes to making decisions. They need community assistance in being firm. If a parent has this problem, it's good for him to have the authority of the church or school to help him take a stand."[4]

Unfortunately, Linzer concedes, some parents lose their sense of responsibility when their authority is taken over by school, church, and the members of the city council (who, if the truth were known, aren't invariably successful at directing young people either).

One contemporary problem is that few fathers earn their livings working near home. Not only is the father gone from home all day, often he has flown to a city hundreds of miles away. Other men of the neighborhood also disappear over the horizon, so children are left to spend their days in a feminine environment. In primitive societies where an approximation of this undesirable situation exists, Yale University researchers have traced some of the results. They discovered an association between cultural patterns that allow young boys to grow up without much contact with their fathers and a high incidence of crime. Enveloped in a feminine milieu, the boys apparently feel obliged to prove their masculinity by acts of revolt—thefts and personal crimes like assaults—against standards they perceive as feminine.[5]

If a father doesn't make up for his absences during the week by spending time with the children over the weekend (as many fathers do), the primitive society in which children live may hand him a few surprises. His boys may make a puberty ritual of burning down the high school or collecting old ladies' purses instead of scalps.

Father's absence is more of an attitude than a division of time. What counts, according to Drs. Ivor Kraft and Catherine Chilman of the U. S. Children's Bureau, is whether the child has some notion of what his father is doing and the security of feeling that in an emergency his father could be reached.[6]

Some fathers no longer feel responsible for their children except financially. Alexander Aldrich, director of the New York State Division of Youth, says many teen-agers, especially in the suburbs, "have to get an appointment" to see their parents at home because every member of the family is constantly busy.[7] Experts blame lack of affection at home as much as any other factor for the soaring rate of illegitimate births to teen-age mothers. Msgr. Daniel A. McGuire, co-administrator of the New York Foundling Hospital, which shelters 3,000 unwed mothers a year, mostly between seventeen and twenty, says: "The girls have a similar history of not feeling loved. Their parents seem a little too busy to show them that they are important members of the family."[8]

Psychological malnutrition has replaced rickets and scurvy as a menace to children, according to Dr. Nathan B. Talbot, Harvard Medical School pediatrician. Although progress in medicine has eliminated many diseases that used to take countless children's lives, nearly forty per cent of young adults now have mental or emotional problems. In the fifteen-to-twenty-five age group, the third and fourth most common causes of death are homicide and suicide, with adolescent suicide rates increasing.[9]

However, it is not at all clear that giving the children more attention automatically makes you a successful parent. If you were doing the wrong things in the first place, more of the same only makes matters worse. A father who hangs around trying to be a pal may secretly be considered a nuisance. A ten-year-old boy whose father often joined the boy and his friends shooting baskets in the driveway was overheard complaining to his mother: "Doesn't Dad have anything else to do? We wish he'd stay in the house so we can play the way we want to."

It isn't possible anyway for a father to devote his entire energy to the family. He must also be the provider, wresting a living from an occupation that is either a considerable psychological drain or doesn't pay much (or both). "Too good" a father may be a poor citizen. As it is now, the world just manages to exist from day to day without collapsing into chaos, thanks to the dedicated efforts of political leaders, educators, preachers, artists, and other men who often have family responsibilities. If a considerable number of them suddenly decided to give up the struggle and devote more time to their children, there wouldn't be anything left for the children to grow up to.

In the life of an individual father, the choices—good father versus good provider versus good citizen—are not presented in abstract purity. Innumerable small decisions have to be made with the basic issues obscured. For instance, there is a strong temptation to adopt a fatherly style which is rationalized as unselfish interest in the child's future when it actually is a form of status seeking.

An increasing number of peptic ulcers are being diagnosed in children as young as seven and eight, stragglers in the lightweight heat of the Rat Race. Psychologists blame parental pressure to achieve, socially and academically. This indirect parental egotism is one reason so many children's lives are crowded with organized activity—music and dancing lessons, Little League, Girl Scouts, park programs—until they have even less leisure than today's harried adults.

Parents can emphasize the wrong values. Dr. Esther Milner of the University of Alberta says a new definition of "good" and "bad" parents has emerged in the middle class. "The good parent places his children's material and physical comfort first and his own second; the not-so-good parent places his own material and physical comfort first and that of his children second."[10]

Unless he is capable of discrimination, the father becomes either a drudge supporting self-centered brats in a style they don't deserve or a ne'er-do-well supporting a convertible or a motorboat in a style he can't afford. "Giving of oneself to one's children," continues Dr. Milner, "during their earlier years . . . has become an actual luxury that many young urban fathers, particularly, feel they cannot afford. Yet such child-attuned giving of self is indispensable for childen's healthy psychological development in our type of family system and our type of society." In some societies, children can sleep in any convenient hut, then stay for a fish and coconut breakfast with their third cousins. We lack these bonus relationships.

Let us now meet a few families who inhabit houses in the kind of block the social sciences can build with research. In the house at the corner live the Twitchys. Clarence Twitchy is a lawyer in the legal department of a large corporation. His wife, Susan, is a full-time editor for a book publisher. A housekeeper cares for their two children. Clarence works under great strain in an office where tension and hostility are the prevailing moods. Susan also works under pressure, with her ego frequently torn up and tossed into the wastebasket by her superiors. Both Clarence and Susan consider their children extensions of their own battered selves. Susan's feelings are complicated by a sense of guilt about working, although she has often declared she couldn't bear to be "just a housewife."

They are both overprotective toward the children. Clarence insists they get high grades in school (higher in fact than he ever received as a boy) and punishes them for any lapses. Susan would not permit them to go to camp or own bicycles because of possible dangers. When once or twice one child or the other has been disciplined in school, Clarence and Susan have descended upon the poor teacher as furious as tigers with a wounded cub.

Both children already are neurotically overanxious. When teasing classmates ditched the boy in a wooded area of a park while on a school outing, he became hysterical.

In the middle of the block live the Cooles. Mr. Coole is intensely absorbed in his career as an executive of a company that puts things in aerosol cans. At the moment they are trying to do it with martini mix. They are having production problems (the olives keep gumming up the nozzles), and he is working nights and sleeping on a cot in his office. Mrs. Coole (none of the neighbors knows their first names) spends her days working for various socially impeccable charity groups and looking for a new house in a more exclusive neighborhood.

A favorite topic of Mrs. Coole's in conversation with her peers is the difficulty of finding housekeepers, a subject on which she is expert because of her impossible boys. The last housekeeper quit because the boys set fire to her blanket one morning when she overslept.

Mrs. Coole occasionally feels remorseful about not spending more time with the boys. Only last summer she regretted sending them to camp for the whole season, especially when they stole the camp truck one night and burned out the transmission trying to tow the camp director's cabin into the lake. She was so upset she almost changed her mind about giving them motorcycles for Christmas.

Mr. Coole never feels guilty. When he thinks about the boys, which isn't often, he tells himself he's working for their future. As for the present, he advised giving them the motorcycles after all because the boys would make such a fuss if they didn't get them. He was right. Lacking genuine parental attention and affection, the boys demand expensive gifts as a substitute. If they had been denied their motorcycles, their reaction would have been far out of proportion. They might have been angry enough to cut the telephone wires again.

Around the corner on a street of much smaller houses is the home of Joe and Sadie Grouch. They both work full-time at a factory in town and Joe works nights as a bartender. Not being able to afford a housekeeper, they allow the children to let themselves in with keys when they arrive home from school. They're supposed to watch television until Sadie finishes her shift and takes the bus home. Joe and Sadie are almost always tired and irritable from overwork. The children usually make a mess in the house during the hour or so they're unsupervised. When they spill peanut butter and jelly on the sofa while watching television and fixing an after-school snack, Sadie is likely to beat them for it upon her arrival.

But the Grouch children don't receive nearly the knocking about the Battersleys are used to. The Battersleys live upstairs over the tavern where Joe Grouch works nights. Ella Battersley has a full-time job at the factory. Her husband, an alcoholic, works irregularly. When in a bad temper, he may beat up everyone in the family. A few months ago he tried to hit the eldest boy with a cast-iron skillet but was too drunk to catch him. That night the boy took all the money in the house and hasn't been heard from since.

These are four of the common patterns of parental failure that psychologists are concerned about. There are others. Symptoms vary according to social class, but in each case the children are consciously or unconsciously rejected. Nothing harms a child more than rejection; nothing can make up to a child for rejection.

In a study of the psychology of character development, R. F. Peck and R. J. Havighurst concluded that "to an almost startling degree, each child learns to feel and act, psychologically and morally, as just the kind of person his father and mother have been in their relationship with him."[11]

Here is a mystery. In the flow of generations can be seen an analogy to the history of salvation. Despite the best efforts of irreproachable parents, some offspring who should be children of light fall from grace like Lucifer and his angels. Also, as with original sin, the absence of emotional and moral maturity in other parents is perpetuated from generation to generation, the parents being unable to give their children that which they do not themselves possess. The cycle of despair would be endless but for redemption which comes from beyond the universe of the individual. Fortunately, there is redemption. Otherwise, how would it be possible to explain the rise of great human beings from unpromising origins?

A distinction must be made between the environment of a child and the child himself. A wise and responsible parent can exert beneficial control over the environment. It has often been shown that homes in which music, art, and conversation are cherished generally produce children who grow up with reverence for reason, beauty, truth, and the other goods of civilization. Parents who instead offer their children vulgar television shows fail them badly.

The same is true of religion. A great many saints have praised the example of their devout parents. And failure to provide a religious atmosphere in the home, in which love of God and trust in Providence are essential elements, is certainly culpable.

But control of the environment is not control of the child, who is a human being with a free will. Each person, at some moment in his life, must resolve the issue of faith on his own. Although he may be the heir of a devout family tradition, he must experience conversion just as if he had been found naked in a pagan jungle by a charismatic missionary, persuaded to give up the bone through his nose, and baptized. Religion that is nothing more than docile acquiescence to family habits is worthless anyway.

"One real conversion in a great city is something more splendid than the spectacle of a whole remote village going to the sacraments," says the noted German theologian, Karl Rahner, S.J. "The one is an essentially religious event, a thing of grace; the other is to a large extent a sociological phenomenon, even though it may be a means of God's grace."[12]

A father gazing upon the faces of his sleeping children may reflect upon his past and their futures with discouragement. It may seem unfair for there to be so many ways for him to fail them while his chances to help them are so limited. If they are healthy, normal children, full of disorganized energy and insubordination, he may think he has already failed beyond hope.

At this point, it is comforting to take Rahner down from the bookshelf once more: "It is precisely for the Christian to hope against hope, knowing that God triumphs when we seem to be lost."[13]

NOTES

1. Frances L. Ilg and Louise Bates Ames, *The Gesell Institute's Child Behavior*. New York: Dell, 1956.
2. *Marriage*, August, 1963.

3. *Science News Letter*, March 16, 1963.

4. *New York Times*, April 8, 1963.

5. *Science News Letter*, June 15, 1963.

6. Samuel Withers, "The 364 Other Days with Father." *New York Times Magazine*, June 16, 1963.

7. *New York Times*, June 6, 1963.

8. *New York Times*, October 3, 1962.

9. *Chicago Daily News*, October 31, 1962.

10. *The Failure of Success*. New York: Exposition, 1959.

11. Karl S. Bernhardt, "Where Does 'Character' Come From?" *New York Times Magazine*, August 25, 1963.

12. *The Christian Commitment*, translated by Cecily Hastings. New York: Sheed & Ward, 1963.

13. *Ibid.*

II

If Your Heart's in the Right Place,
Your Foot's in Your Mouth

Sunday morning. As I wake and squint at the clock, trying to decide whether to leap up NOW to go to church or yield to my true character by flopping back down and waiting for a later Mass, I gradually become aware of a guilty gray cast to the light of morning. Then I begin to remember the reason I feel unworthy for the sun to shine on. There was a party last night, and I was talking.

By now my wife has one eye open. "Did I talk too much last night?" I ask her. "Did I say anything I shouldn't have?" These are rhetorical questions with only one possible answer. The only way I could have been saved was for her to have really talked too much and held the floor all evening. Either way, between us we have failed socially one more time.

With the hydrogen bomb and everything else to worry about, it may seem frivolous to be concerned about social success or failure. But this is a pose or a misunderstanding.

Everyone needs friends. The misunderstanding may arise from confusing friends with acquaintances. A friend is someone who is still friendly after he has had a chance to get to know the real you. You can talk too much in the presence of a friend and it won't make any difference. Or not much. In any case, a friend sooner or later forgives. No one can have too many friends. Acquaintances can, in some circumstances, be far too numerous.

To develop a friendship ordinarily requires a major investment of time over a period of years. Because there isn't time to cultivate a large crop of friends, the total usually remains small. Friendship can grow only in a climate of intimacy, which cannot be sustained by occasional dinner parties unless there is a rare degree of natural rapport. We tend to mask our real selves from each other. Even if one of the members of a would-be friendship is adept at mask-dropping, the other may not notice without repeated exposures.

Cultivating friends is more difficult than it used to be. Nowadays, about the time you finally begin to warm up to someone, and vice versa, he moves—to New York City if you live in the sticks or out to the sticks if you live in New York. And we don't seem to have the time for the long, long conversations that either drive off an acquaintance entirely or turn him into a friend.

Friends give us more than we realize. Besides the comforting in distress and rejoicing in our good fortune for which we all appreciate friends, they improve our characters. If we are about to make a serious mistake, a friend may be the only person who dares point it out, and the only person whose reproach would be persuasive. Friends teach us to practice the works of mercy, because being kind to a friend seems only natural and, with repeated opportunities, we may find it habit-forming. Having friends develops our own capacity for loving, which is the most important quality of human personality.

"Modern man is alienated from himself, from his fellow men, and from nature," says Erich Fromm. "He has been transformed into a commodity, experiences his life forces as an investment which must bring him the maximum profit obtainable," which fact he hides from himself through "bureaucratized, mechanical work. . . . passive consumption of sounds and sights offered by the amusement industry" and the "satisfaction of buying ever new things."[1]

This theme is important in literature, too. *The Zoo Story*, the play that first brought dramatist Edward Albee to prominence, is about a man named Jerry who is alienated. Jerry, in a desperate attempt to establish any kind of human contact just once in his life, goads a mild-mannered textbook editor into killing him.

On bad days, the newspaper headlines create the impression that the whole country, the whole world is alienated. This can't be true. Some of the people still have friends, and a man with friends is never alienated, no matter how many other frustrations society exposes him to.

Acquaintances range from the friendly waitress at your favorite restaurant to someone on the verge of joining the select circle of your friends. A person doesn't need acquaintances as much as he needs friends, but to be realistic, it must be admitted that acquaintances come in handy. In business, acquaintanceships of the better sort are referred to as "contacts." They can help you find a job, sell your house, gather useful information, and make things happen. To exploit contacts is crass. However, if you are raising funds for a worthy cause, seeking some reform in the community, or trying to find work for an unemployed relative who has been borrowing money from you, it is best to go to a man with contacts.

A wide circle of acquaintances is stimulating, exposing the possessor to manners, tastes, and ideas that might not otherwise come his way. The person is rare who limits his social intercourse to a handful of true friends and devotes none of his time to the company of acquaintances. The kind of social life that is parodied in fiction because it is so rife with opportunities for failure involves acquaintances rather than friends. You don't need a gimmick to remember the name of a friend (at least, not very often). Nor do you have to give a friend the impression that he was first on the guest list to be invited, a gambit that sits well with acquaintances. One of the most important reasons for encouraging acquaintances is that they often become friends in time.

Friends not only have to be developed; unfortunately, they occasionally have to be replaced. All of us sometimes place strains on friendship that are too strong for the bond. Another way to define friendship is to say that neither of the friends is using the other somehow to improve his position in the world.

Everyone knows Joe Porifera, the neighborhood sponge, or his equivalent. Joe apparently keeps a notebook on what his contacts might be able to do for him someday. If your company manufactures something he can use, he'll be on the phone inquiring whether you can get him a wholesale price. And he has put away at least half a case of your Scotch since the last time you were invited to his house.

Then there's Ella Potlatch. If you admire anything at her house, she takes it off the wall and gives it to you. She never comes to visit without an expensive gift. You have no alternative but to be drawn into a costly game of oneupmanship or to feel always like a poor relative.

And if you resent either of them, you blame your own defects of character: you wouldn't mind Joe but for being stingy yourself; Ella only bothers you because you're too proud.

Steve Snivet is a different kind of problem. He comes to your house, roosts in the most comfortable chair, and says nothing. He answers direct questions "Yes," "No," or "I couldn't say," which is one of his longer speeches. Snivet takes the starch out of a party like a thundershower at a parish barbecue. You wouldn't invite him anymore but for the embarrassing fact that he likes you.

Bill Bison is the opposite. Bill comes on like a tape-recorded monolog. He never gives you or anyone else a chance to say anything unless he accidentally chokes on a canapé. You once thought Snivet and Bison were perfectly matched guests, but it turned out that Snivet loathes Bison and goes home early whenever he finds him at a party.

Dealing with acquaintances has certain character-building aspects. Hospitality, for instance, is one of the virtues. St. Benedict, in his celebrated rule, made a point of saying, "Let all guests. . . . be received as Christ Himself." There are shocking transgressions today of the hospitable tradition. A special agency has sprung up in New York that employs housewives to deliver commercials to friends and acquaintances as they circulate at club meetings and other gatherings, keeping track with a pocket-sized meter of the number of commercials inserted in their conversations.[2] And several industries are built on the idea of having a housewife invite her neighbors in for a sales pitch by a salesman, who gives the hostess a cut of the proceeds.

In a social encounter, a person has responsibilities that cannot be shucked off as easily as a second helping of a misconceived casserole. The host must try to see that everyone feels welcome and entertained. A guest has an obligation to allow himself to be entertained, even to participate in the entertainment of other guests. It is wrong of him to spend the evening hidden shyly in the shrubbery on the flowered wallpaper or standing as stiff as a marble bust within arm's reach of the bar, waiting to be amused.

What I am talking about is more than good manners. It involves both justice and charity. Justice because of the tacit contract between host and guests. The host could have saved his Scotch for a happier occasion and gone to bed early with a good book. The guests could have chosen to attend a better blowout or, lacking an invitation, gone to the movies. Since each party to the contract has made an investment in the evening, the other is bound to contribute something towards its success.

Charity is involved because people nowadays can express love for each other more readily in social situations than in other areas of life. The various forms of alms-giving have

become institutionalized. During working hours imper-
sonal forces beyond the control of individuals regulate
much of what happens. But, at a party, if you willingly
suffer a bore to come unto you for half an hour, you have
freely performed a work of charity. The world is full of
sad people whose burdens can be briefly lightened by a
sympathetic ear. Any kind of ear for that matter. Hearing
them out is not always the jolliest way to spend your time,
but great is your reward in heaven.

A still greater challenge to character, of course, is your
response to the sudden realization that someone who considers YOU a bore is giving you the patient treatment.

There are many ways to spread sunshine. Once I was
invited to an open house by a young reporter who had just
moved into a new apartment. The same invitation was extended to other members of the staff of the paper we
worked for, and I assumed there would be a considerable
turnout. On the night of the party, I happened to run into
a couple of friends who insisted on having a drink. Because
of the "crowd" at the open house, I didn't feel obligated to
get there on time, and might not have got there at all but
for upbringing that made it a reflex to appear wherever one
had accepted an invitation. I finally persuaded the friends
to accompany me, pointing out that the party was an open
house rather than an intimate dinner for which the pork
chops had been counted.

En route to the remote suburb where the party was
being held, we took the wrong road a couple of times.
With one thing and another, it was after ten o'clock when
we arrived. We found the host and his recent bride sitting

alone in despair beside a whole ham and enough other food and refreshment for a Polish wedding and Irish wake combined. Through a series of coincidences—no baby sitters, car trouble, previous plans—not one of the others invited had appeared.

By arriving more or less accidentally with reinforcements, I had made a party possible after all. Never again in a lifetime will I be able to do that man so great a kindness.

In the effort to be outgoing in social situations, you are as likely as not to make a fool of yourself. You try to smooth over an awkward moment with a joke, and no one else thinks it's funny. You strike up a conversation with a woman no one is talking to, and she begins telling you things about her husband you shouldn't be hearing. You'll regret it all in the morning. But the alternative is to withdraw from human contacts entirely. That's the only sure way to avoid saying something you'll brood about later.

There is a certain asceticism to social life. A person can't spend all his time at it. Like a child at a candy counter, he must study the goodies available and choose wisely. In some circles, it is too easy to fall into a routine of weekend parties. A drink with the neighbors on Friday, dinner with friends on Saturday, company drops in on Sunday, then it's Monday and back to work. These are the people who wonder why they never have time to read or think.

At the opposite extreme are those with a use for solitude, such as writers, who consider all forms of social life a drain on their creative powers and contrive ingenious excuses to avoid being invited anywhere.

Obviously, if you overdo the hermit pose, you gradually

lose whatever friends you may have had. Even the most loyal friend has to be cultivated from time to time or he'll take up with another crowd. On the other hand, too much of the same friend can be too much. Thoreau makes the point somewhere that friends should not gather for conversation too frequently because between meetings they will not have had the time to read, experience, and think enough to give them anything worthwhile to say to each other. This is why men who work together and lunch together every day seldom can find anything to talk about beyond what was on television last night.

Whether a person is naturally as gregarious as a mosquito or is driven by inner discontent to seek company, he can easily fritter away time in social intercourse that rightfully belongs to his family. For a man, this is a special temptation when the entertaining involves business contacts. He can rationalize the neglect, telling himself that keeping close to the customers is part of his duty as breadwinner. For a woman, the temptation lurks on the bridge and committee circuit, where women often can find recognition as individuals which is denied them elsewhere.

This last remark is not intended as a sneer at the volunteer organizations which are so important to our national life. However, the stimulation of being out in company with a new audience for your old jokes and new shoes for self-confidence is one reason why people join even the most dedicated groups.

Choice opportunities for failure are as omnipresent in volunteer organizations as chicken à la king and peas. The purpose of any such organization obviously relates to some shared interest of the members. Preserving something that ought to be preserved. Encouraging something that needs encouraging. Raising funds for a good cause. The whole membership can be dipped in failure when the organization is unable to reach its goals.

There can be various reasons for total failure. The problem can be too hard, as in the case of committees trying to prove Shakespeare's plays were really written by the plans board at Bacon & Jonson. Or the problem can disappear. A few devoted animal lovers still support the Anti-Cruelty Society, but its past success in obtaining anti-cruelty legislation has greatly circumscribed its work today.

Organizations may fail because no leader appears who is willing to do more than his fair share of the work. No organization composed solely of the mildly interested has ever accomplished anything. There always has to be at least one work-horse who does half the work himself and shames, wheedles, and drives the rest of the members to do the other half.

A person can throw himself into the work of an organization because he sincerely identifies with its goals. Let us imagine a Society for the Preservation of Individualistic Traits (SPIT). The president is an idealist who has made many sacrifices for the cause of individualism, and his personal life and character are rather an inspiration to the rank and file.

The vice president is one of those joiners who enjoy acquiring power and a title in any way possible, even if it's only the Veep of SPIT. Significantly, he has not been very successful in his occupation, and his efforts in SPIT are obviously a compensation for his other failures.

The organization also boasts its compulsive aggressive, who is the membership chairman. This man has been successful at everything he ever tried, since the day he became the long-distance spitting champion of North Elm Street. He thinks of SPIT as competing against other volunteer organizations and gives it the same kind of drive that has put him out ahead in business. He is a great asset.

Many members of the organization are aware that not all the officers have pure motives, but they don't much care. Whether an organization is purely social or exists to raise funds for retarded children and indigent old folks, we are always glad to find members who have any kind of motive that makes them work.

Motives are always mixed, of course, Even the most dedicated do-gooders can't resist taking pleasure in creative accomplishment. To have made order out of chaos, created an answer to an unmet need, and solved complex problems is pleasing in itself. Many truly significant changes in society have been achieved through the work of volunteer organizations, and these changes become monuments to the men and women who wrought them.

Organizations fail most of all because of failure in human relationships—the same kinds of failures we are all involved in from time to time at home, in business, on the street. There is failure to recognize or consider the personal motives of others. The chairman, Clarence Quaver, gets up to speak, and—choked with emotion—proclaims the need for sacrifices by all loyal members. It's no sacrifice for him. If anything is accomplished, he'll get all the credit. Or leaders become preoccupied with their own needs. Frank "Front Page" Figley contrives to have himself elected publicity chairman year after year until the younger members who should be receiving training and gradually increased responsibility give up in disgust, to the detriment of the organization and its goals.

But just because members of such groups expect to enjoy a certain amount of socializing while putting over the referendum or revitalizing the parish there is no reason to say that many of them have questionable motives: getting ahead socially, escaping the dullness of their spouses, fleeing from boredom generally. In or out of organizations, many people enjoy true friendships, and to spend their time with congenial companions and work together for some cause is certainly not compensating for failure.

The member of numerous organizations should occasionally ask himself whether he is giving himself enough unhurried, thoughtful leisure time in which to develop whatever intellectual and spiritual potential he possesses. This is a thought that comes easily to the introvert who perhaps would be better off with more, not less, social involvement. For an extrovert to grasp it requires lengthy, patient explanation.

The overactive person, constantly exercising the social graces in dealings with others, tends to allow a stifling degree of conformity to be imposed on him. For instance, it is said to be bad manners to discuss controversial topics at social gatherings. Yet, controversial topics are the only ones worth talking about. People know this, and you can't be with an alert, informed group long before you hear a definite stand being taken on politics, foreign affairs, books, or some other subject about which you feel obliged to straighten out the speaker before his incredibly wrong-headed opinions are disseminated further (to the peril of the Republic). Charity says, "Let it pass, let it pass." Justice says, "Speak out," for the truth is a mighty sword that may not be sheathed.

Anyone who has never offended either charity or justice under circumstances like these may not be a social failure, but he's some other kind of failure for sure.

NOTES

1. *The Art of Loving.* New York: Harper & Row, 1956.
2. *New York Times,* September 11, 1963.

12

How to Fail As a Failure

Success can't be all bad. Some of my best friends have been quite successful in corporations and other high-casualty combat areas while remaining admirable in all respects and an inspiration to their biographers.

They are not the only ones resisting the usual pressures. Among the competitively aggressive neurotics and other reptilian species in top jobs a new kind of manager is beginning to appear, labeled the "Renaissance executive." The American Management Association, in a *New York Times* advertising supplement, described the new business leader as "a sort of twentieth-century universal man. . . . Breadth, as a matter of fact, is an essential of chief executives of large corporations."[1] *Newsweek* has named five men it considers worthy of being listed as Renaissance executives for their breadth of mind and social consciences. They are Fairfax Cone, of Foote, Cone & Belding, advertising agency; Thomas J. Watson Jr., IBM chairman; Thomas Jones, chairman of Northrup Corp.; Richard Cross, chairman of American Motors; and Leonard McCollum, president of Continental Oil. To this group I would add Crawford H. Greenewalt, an engineer who found time to become an expert ornithologist and wildlife photographer while working up to chairman of the board at DuPont. I am especially charmed by an executive with the courage to write a definitive study of hummingbirds under his own name.

According to a survey by *Scientific American*, men with scientific and engineering backgrounds will fill more than half the top management jobs in United States corporations by 1980.[2] Whether this trend will produce more Renaissance executives remains to be seen. Scientific and engineering education during the years the top men of 1980 were in school often was criticized for producing narrow specialists rather than modern Leonardo da Vincis.

I don't think this book will make me popular with ordinary executives, whose Renaissance tendencies may be more Machiavellian than Michelangelic. They can't be expected to agree with my occupational pacifism. Still, I am not utterly subversive regarding the usual organization values. I have to give the typical manager credit for what he does.

Somehow, he brings large groups of disparate, clashing personalities into a *modus vivendi* that permits the organization to contribute its goods or services towards the needs of society. David W. Ewing, of the *Harvard Business Review*, in his book *The Managerial Mind*, defines the managerial type as committed to the survival and growth of the organization for its own sake. Someone has to care. Unless an enterprise can achieve and maintain excellence in some area of operation, its competitors sooner or later will do it in.

The manager has an important role outside of business, too. Scholars and teachers, for instance, mutter about the former accountants, salesmen, and generals who become college presidents, without facing the fact that a scholarly mind may or may not be skilled at coping with two deans who never speak to each other and a state legislature that is singularly boobish this session.

For the man with the right combination of luck and ability to fail as a failure by rising to leadership in the organizational world, the moral challenge is age-old: to escape the corrupting influence of power. When Theodore Roosevelt was President of the United States he continued to attend meetings of his Masonic lodge in Oyster Bay, New York. The master of the lodge was the gardener on the estate of one of Roosevelt's cousins. The President, who enjoyed his friendships with ordinary folk, explained to a local minister: "When I visit the lodge he (the gardener) is my boss, and I must stand up when he orders me, and sit down when he tells me, and not speak unless he allows me. That's good for him and good for me."[3] A big thought from the Big Stick.

For most of the rest of us, failing as failures means falling back on the classic sour grapes defense mechanism. If we give up kicking and gouging to get ahead, we immediately announce virtuously that we didn't want to be a nasty old vice president anyway. But nobody believes it.

David Riesman, the Harvard sociologist, fears that to-day's college students are inclined to play it too cool.

> In the course of getting rid of earlier collegiate or rah-rah enthusiasm, these young people have come to feel that work is not worth even their part-time devotion, and perhaps that nothing, except the family, deserves their wholehearted allegiance. . . . believing that every occupation is a racket and that at best some of the racketeers are less pious about it than others.[4]

He observes that these students allow themselves to be put upon by authority more than is necessary, each in his isolation thinking he is the only one who would object if he could.

The Rev. Thomas M. Garrett, S.J., in his studies of business ethics, sees another aspect of the same problem.

> Too often the really talented man allows himself to become trapped into running minor affairs in his church or community and so neglects those areas of business where he could make a truly significant contribution to society.[5]

There's a grain of truth in the Communist charge that religion has been used as an opiate to dull people to problems that could be solved by ingenuity and diligence. A certain false other-worldliness has provided some individuals with an excuse to escape responsibility.

Never taste of the sour grape; it is deadlier than hemlock.

Any discussion of organization life eventually comes round to the tension between authority and freedom, which has been debated with notable sensitivity by the Protestant theologian Reinhold Niebuhr and Kenneth E. Boulding, professor of economics at the University of Michigan. "Even in the family some coercion is used to preserve order and harmony against recalcitrant tendencies," says Niebuhr, who without condoning tyranny defends the necessary exercise of authority in modern organizations.[6] Boulding fears the coercive nature of these organizations. He says:

> I may sum up the difference a little ruthlessly by saying that Professor Niebuhr is afraid of freedom, seeing always behind it the specter of anarchy; whereas I am afraid of justice, seeing always behind it the specter of tyranny. The difference between us is perhaps the difference between the Lutheran vision of God as Mighty Fortress and the Quaker vision of God as the Living Seed. That both these visions describe a vital religious experience can hardly be doubted. The former I appreciate intellectually; the latter I claim as my own.[7]

The analogy between the politics of government and the politics of other organizations has been suggested by many observers. Over the centuries we have evolved a system of government that does rather well at balancing freedom and authority. Most of our citizens enjoy a degree of freedom seldom dreamed of throughout most of recorded history.

Those who have not shared fully in these rights in the past now have the authority of the government on their side. The machinery for securing desirable changes may creak and groan and rattle at times, but it works.

Not so with concentrated economic power. We are still experimenting with ways to reconcile freedom and authority within corporations.

One approach has been government regulation. The public considers it proper for the government to prevent honest corporations from having their throats cut by pirates. The public also appreciates the government's efforts in prohibiting criminally inclined corporations from picking the pockets of the citizenry. But the power of the state cannot be extended indefinitely without threatening the hard-won liberties mentioned above. When the feds confiscate a shipment of mislabeled drugs, that's quite a different case from having a government agent sit in at every meeting of every management committee.

The other principal response to economic power has been the labor movement. Old-time capitalistic theory held that wages should be determined by supply and demand. It was assumed that one worker was freely exchangeable for any other worker; therefore, if a company could find takers for jobs paying $7 a week, that's as much as they'd offer anyone. In winning a bargaining position for labor, unions tacitly accepted the same assumption about the interchangeability of workers. It is the power of the union that shields the workers from exploitation and mistreatment rather than the company's need for any particular worker or workers.

Supervisory employees, who are the ones upon whom the pressures we have been discussing lie heaviest, traditionally have been excluded from coverage by union contracts for two reasons. The first, that they are supposed to be more loyal to the management than the union men, ought to be re-examined every time an executive is caught taking kickbacks from suppliers or cheating outrageously on his expense account. The second, that they have individual bargaining power based on their skills, is partly true. At least some of the supervisers and staff experts earning five-figure salaries must earn what they get or the organizations employing them wouldn't be prosperous enough to pay up.

This being the case, why do employees of this type allow themselves to be pushed around? There are unethical practices that trouble men's consciences about their own company or their industry. Also, there are individual outrages, like snooping personality tests, arbitrary and frequent transfers to distant cities, and management meddling in personal affairs.

These things would not happen if there were more stubborn, independent spirits who simply said "No." As it is, the independent spirit finds himself quickly replaced by someone more flexible while his relatives and neighbors regard him as a nut.

The unionization of management is a possible but unlikely solution. Imagine the scene when a grievance committee from the Vice Presidents' and Executive Understudies' Union is admitted to the office of the president of the Interplanetary Corporation.

"What's the grievance, boys?" says the president.

"You can't transfer John Beaver to the Bangkok branch," says Hector Gladly, chairman of the committee. "The contract provides that no vice president can be transferred with less than a year's notice."

The president has an answer ready. "I know it's rough on Beaver, but we're reorganizing. As a matter of fact, Gladly, we're thinking of transferring some of Beaver's responsibilities to your division. And, Strively, we were going to have you fill in for Beaver in the office here. But if the contract says—"

The committee instantly recognizes where its duty lies. Gladly elbows Strively, who volunteers: "I'll be happy to drive Mr. Beaver to the airport after five o'clock, Mr. Bigley."

Another possible control measure is the development of a system of political checks and balances within the organization. At present, political life in corporations has progressed to about the level of a comic opera banana republic. For instance, when the Out faction stages a palace revolt and becomes the In faction, one of the first things they do is line up the advertising against a wall and execute the agency hired by the deposed party. Barbaric!

It is possible to hope for a more progressive corporate political climate in the future. Extension of the two-party system to elections for the board of directors would make stockholders more interested in the company. Instead of Democrats and Republicans, there could be the Higher Equities versus the Cash Nows. The board would have to include a Catholic, a Jew, an Italian, a Pole, and a Negro, increasing employment opportunities for minorities.

If employees as well as stockholders were given votes, we'd see good old American political know-how going to town. Meet-the-candidate teas for the ladies of the stenographic pool. Pork barrel promises, like a new and bigger laboratory for the research department, maybe in Florida. If you're late for work, your department precinct captain can fix it up. Speeches in the company cafeteria, with always at least one conservative candidate to add color by proposing a return to making things by hand or an improvement in the company's share of market to be won by putting a bomb in the chief competitor's plant.

Nothing is likely to change so long as supervisory employees of the organization are vulnerable to hints from management that they may someday win promotion if they never complain about anything, no matter how unreasonable. Inordinate hunger for promotion isolates the individual and prevents him from combining with others for mutual benefit. In moral terms, the only successful way to be successful is to work hard, but not too hard; to head for the top, but not at top speed; and arrive at power, not by seizing it, but by accepting it when offered.

This is the hard way, so you will probably fail, just as I've been warning you all along.

Norman Podhoretz, the editor of *Commentary*, has detected a current of sad resignation running through contemporary television drama as a consistent theme. The people reflected in these plays, like Riesman's college students, play it cool. The object of ambition becomes not success but mature acceptance of reality, conquest not of circumstances but of self. The note of sadness is struck, Podhoretz says, because of the realization that this kind of success is just as elusive as any other.

> When success is measured by money or fame, failure can be chalked up to bad luck; the whole man is rarely in the balance, for a certain distinction will be maintained between the private and public selves: the private self is there to fall back upon if the other turns out treacherous. But when success is conceived as an attribute of the personality rather than of the wallet, failure becomes the tenth circle of Hell.[8]

Happily married husbands and wives, parents whose children are still a credit to them at the age of thirty, beloved community leaders who have innumerable warm friends and never say the wrong thing to any of them—all confront us with the proof of our own intangible failures.

So there it is—you've failed in the world, failed at home, failed as a personality. You're a failure to the marrow of your bone. The ultimate test, then, is whether failure makes you bitter. The truth is that failure is a joke, not for the derision of demons, but the gentle laughter of the saints.

NOTES

1. September 15, 1963.
2. *Chicago Daily News,* June 25, 1964.
3. Hermann Hagedorn, *The Roosevelt Family of Sagamore Hill.* New York: Macmillan, 1954.
4. *The Dilemma of Organizational Society,* edited by Hendrik M. Ruitenbeek. New York: Dutton, 1963.
5. *Ethics in Business.* New York: Sheed & Ward, 1963.
6. *The Organizational Revolution: A Study in the Ethics of Economic Organization.* New York: Harper, 1953.
7. *Ibid.*
8. *Doings and Undoings: the fifties and after in American writing.* New York: Farrar, Straus, 1964.